A Year in the
Country

A Year in the Country

ASSOCIATE CREATIVE DIRECTOR
Christina Spalatin
DEPUTY EDITORS Marija Andric,
Jennifer Zeigler
ART DIRECTOR Kristen Stecklein
ASSOCIATE EDITOR Molly Jasinski
LAYOUT DESIGNERS Joe Hrdina,
Samantha Williams
COPY EDITOR Ann Walter
PRODUCTION COORDINATOR
Jon Syverson
SENIOR RIGHTS ASSOCIATE Jill Godsey

FRONT COVER Craggy Gardens,
Dave Allen Photography
TITLE PAGE Carrizo Plain National
Monument, Terry Donnelly

© 2020 RDA Enthusiast Brands, LLC.
1610 N. 2nd St., Suite 102
Milwaukee, WI 53212-3906

International Standard Book Number
978-1-61765-910-2 (dated),
978-1-61765-911-9 (undated)
International Standard Serial Number
2576-3679
Component Number
116800025H (dated),
116800027H (undated)

TABLE OF CONTENTS

Come On In...

Created to be a true reflection of life in the country, this book showcases what really matters—living in harmony with nature, appreciating the value of hard work, and cherishing fond moments with the people you love.

A Year in the Country celebrates the everyday occurrences, heartwarming stories and candid photos from the readers of *Country, Farm & Ranch Living, Country Woman* and *Birds & Blooms* magazines. These treasured memories reveal the beauty of America's great outdoors, the bonds of community, the importance of family traditions and so much more.

Page through the book, divided by season, and discover comforting recipes, creative crafts to share, stories that will touch your heart and remind you of times gone by, and stunning photography of farm life, animals and gorgeous landscapes.

We hope you feel the serenity of the country as you look through this collection of the past year's best moments.

—The Editors

Fresh blooms signal the start of a new season at Magnolia Plantation and Gardens in Charleston, South Carolina.
PHOTO BY DAVE ALLEN PHOTOGRAPHY/SHUTTERSTOCK

Spring

Horsefeathers Ranch

When her parents bought 40 acres in the Arizona desert,
she discovered a land that made her spirit soar.

BY JENNIFER WILSON *Taylor, Arizona*

Growing up, my sisters and I always longed to live in the country. So when my parents chose to move to a small rural community north of the White Mountains of Arizona, we were thrilled. By then we were all in our late teens and early 20s, but we eagerly jumped at the opportunity to help our parents create a haven away from the city.

Wanting to experience the true rural life, my parents purchased 40 acres of land about an hour from any town. The property had been dubbed "Horsefeathers Ranch" by previous owners and we kept it.

The house hadn't been lived in for 10 years. Undaunted by a decade's worth of mouse excrement and dead bugs, we all pitched in cleaning and sweeping.

For a few weeks, we let out piercing screams as we ran into creatures of the area. Moths and spiders bothered my sisters, but I was more troubled after my first encounter with a centipede. And mice had us all jumping.

I liked the horned toads that blinked lazily in the sun, and I grabbed my camera to try to get a good shot of the bullsnakes in Mom's garden. I found tarantulas fascinating and even kind of cute.

Raised by a dad who didn't think twice about giving his girls a tool or a hammer, we got to work, laying tile and grouting, hanging drywall, and endlessly painting. Every night we collapsed, so exhausted we could hardly sleep, only to get up and do it again the next day.

Jennifer (above) smiles by a 1971 Dodge work truck.

The family home (far left) offers unobstructed views of the sky (top) in all directions. Continuing clockwise: rabbits and critters galore make the desert their home; Dad sits at the "phone booth"; a prairie coneflower blooms.

It was worth it. The dramatic changes going on inside the house were matched by spectacular vistas outside, and every chance I could get, I explored our property.

To the east was a stand of juniper trees so thick you had to walk almost all the way around to get into the heart of them, where there was cool shade. On the other side of the trees was a deep sandy area, so soft and smooth it felt like a beach. Everywhere else the earth was red, with the prettiest rocks waiting to be discovered.

I loved to wander, with only the sound of the wind and my footsteps for company. I found giant logs of petrified wood, and even a petroglyph carved into a boulder, showing that the history of this land includes an ancient people who wanted to leave their mark.

We weren't connected to any power lines, phone lines or city water. The house was powered by a generator supplemented by solar panels and a wind machine that Dad added. The energy they generated was stored in batteries for use overnight, and we quickly learned to check the power before using a hair dryer.

Only one spot on the whole 40 acres seemed to work for a cellphone, and luckily it was right outside the house. My dad put a lawn chair there, and we ended up dubbing it "The Phone Booth."

> I loved to wander, with only the sound of the wind and my own footsteps for company.

The lessons of living in the high mountain deserts were many. I learned coyotes don't always howl mournfully but very often yelp and laugh. If you lie down to rest under a tree in the midst of hiking, the ravens will circle overhead. And the desert can produce flowers as delicate and perfect as any in a flower shop.

I revel in this strange, dusty, beautiful place that God made with so much creativity. If you are looking for some soft greenery and rushing streams, then the Arizona desert is not for you. But if you appreciate the red earth, bounding jack rabbits and the fresh smell of juniper trees, then you have found a place to give your soul joy. ☀

Virginia uses the shed for both storage and relaxation.

A Special Little Shed

Her garden oasis allows for reflection and new memories.

BY VIRGINIA RATHERT ZETTERBERG *Jefferson, Maryland*

My husband and I designed and built my little garden shed in 2009 as a place of refuge and relaxation.

We decided to construct it using many recycled elements: the old front door from a friend's house; extra siding from our next-door neighbor's home; screen windows from a garage sale; and some roof shingles from two other projects on our property.

Although the little garden shed is now a decade old, it embodies a much longer history. In addition to the structure's recycled elements, I've used some old curtains from my childhood bedroom and a table and chair from our former audio and video recording company office. Many of the contents, both useful and decorative, have been handed down or gifted from our family and friends. Even though I'm usually alone in my shed, I always feel the presence of these dear people. It is my sanctuary.

Nestled beneath the pine trees just a few feet from our front porch, it is a refuge I try to visit most days. Even though we got 32 inches of snow in one day a few years ago, I still dug my way to the shed to be sure everything was OK out there. It was. An ice storm the previous year brought down numerous pine limbs but left the shed unscathed. It has truly been a shelter in the storm.

Since it's relatively cool and bug-free in the warmer

Clockwise from left: Virginia's husband, Don, helped build the shed in 2009. Shelves hold gardening books, while the walls provide good spots for hanging tools and hats. The bulletin board displays Virginia's annual vegetable garden layout, along with a calendar and thermometer.

months, the shed is a welcome retreat from garden work. It's a place to pull out books, make plans, try to resolve problems, sip a cold drink or enjoy an early morning cup of coffee with just the sounds of the birds and the small waterfall in our nearby pond. It's so peaceful to watch the birds and squirrels flitting and scampering around, seemingly unaware of my presence.

I learn a lot of lessons in both my garden and my shed. Occasionally I sit quietly in my shed and write down a few of them. There is one lesson I did not write down but certainly won't forget. The shed was new and a short ramp to the door was covered with pine needles. I kept telling myself I needed to sweep them away—soon. But I didn't do it soon enough, and one day I slid off the ramp and broke my ankle. Some lessons you learn the hard way! I sweep the pine needles frequently now.

Organizing space is one of my joys, and arranging an 8-by-12-foot structure dedicated to gardening pursuits has been easy to accomplish. Unlike our home, where I frequently redesign and repurpose rooms, the shed is stable. Reminders of our accomplishments are visible when I look out the windows. We took out five overgrown Leyland cypress trees this spring, in addition to digging up zebra grass and replanting it where the trees had been. The pond, visible from another window, was a point of frustration this spring when we couldn't find the source of a serious leak. Now it's resolved and the pond once again is a relaxing sight.

As the years go by, this little structure becomes even more special to me. This former city girl's heart has found a new home here in the Maryland countryside, and in my cozy potting shed. ☀

The Bunkhouse

One special building brought family, history and design together.

BY SETH KULAS *Edwards, Colorado*

Like most worthwhile projects, the idea behind our family's Bunkhouse started small. We just needed time, passion and good old-fashioned elbow grease to finally convert our vision into something tangible. With creative plans and bodies able and ready, that idea manifested into a labor of love that lasted two years.

My great-grandparents purchased our family farm in 1923, and they chose a pristine plot. Occupying 175 acres of prime Wisconsin earth, the farm had it all: a meandering stream that's home to healthy trout; hardwood forests; views of the Mississippi River Valley; abundant wildlife; and large swaths of highly tillable black soil. It offered a chance for their American dreams to grow. They were dairy farmers living the good life in what they refer to as "God's country."

My parents eventually renovated the farmhouse, adding another bedroom and ample floor space, but the accommodations were still a little cramped when the entire family—which had grown to 17 over the years—gathered there. The grandkids slept strewn about the

From far left: Located on the Kulas family farm in Wisconsin, the Bunkhouse took two years of hard work to construct; the Kulas family together at Seth's recent wedding; Seth's mom added little lanterns above each bunk bed for pre-nap story times with the grandkids; reclaimed pinewood flooring greets Bunkhouse visitors.

living room floor. GiGi, my grandma (who is now great-grandmother to seven) lived in a home several hundred yards away and always offered her extra bedroom up as overflow until she moved to an assisted-living facility several years ago.

But as the kids got bigger and the family gatherings became more frequent, the idea of a humble Bunkhouse was born. My brother-in-law Chuck drew up a rough sketch of a lean-to style structure, floorless and largely open to the elements, where he envisioned the kids would camp out during the warmer months. But since we're not really a family of campers (except for myself), we refined Chuck's original idea, adding walls, a heat source and a few other luxuries.

Hundreds, if not thousands, of hours went into the planning, building and outfitting the Bunkhouse. My mom is an artist, as crafty as they get, and radiates creativity. My dad is a jack-of-all-trades, a hardcore DIYer and a seasoned problem-solver. With these unique qualities, my mom's imaginative vision materialized through my dad's craftsmanship. Together, they made the idea of the Bunkhouse a reality.

Construction began in June 2015. It started with pouring a 26-by-26-foot concrete slab and digging a trench from the farmhouse to the Bunkhouse pad for electrical and plumbing lines. Props to my pops, as he personally built 90 percent of the Bunkhouse—using just a handful of tools—while the rest of us helped as we could. I set the trusses onto the framing with my dad and three brothers-in-law; my two nephews helped secure the subflooring to the foundation; and my mom power-washed hundreds of boards of reclaimed wainscoting. The Bunkhouse was finally completed and ready for visitors in November 2017.

There are many details that make the Bunkhouse special: the French door entrance; a loft with a fencelike oak partition; a ceiling made from reclaimed oak rafters; and bunk beds that double as a jungle gym for the kids. It has vintage furniture from my mom's parents in the living room, and there's a vanity in the bathroom that my dad constructed out of an old hay wagon. My mom added her artistic touch by painting throughout the house. If you gaze out the bedroom window, you may catch a glimpse of a white-tailed deer, ring-necked pheasants or sandhill cranes.

Our family came together to build something beautiful and astonishing. It's teeming with history, full of refined details and overflowing with purpose. We'll cherish the Bunkhouse for many generations to come. ☀

From top: The bathroom vanity was made by Seth's dad out of an old hay wagon. At a local antique shop, Seth's mom found the vintage desk that now sits just inside the front door. The loft offers extra space for little ones to play or sleep on air mattresses and in sleeping bags.

Myrtle, Wanda, Mini and LilBit scratch the ground and search for bugs.

Walking with the Girls

Four feisty hens love to stretch their legs every day.

BY LAURA RUST *Coleman, Texas*

While I was out walking my Dominique chickens, one of them started "killing" something. Since it was a cold day, I knew no sane bug would be traipsing about, so I went to investigate.

I glimpsed a rubber band in Myrtle's beak, and then the chase was on! Wanda, Mini and LilBit (especially LilBit) were all after her to get the prize, and I was after them.

As each chicken dropped the rubber band, the next one picked it up and ran with it. With this middle-aged woman bringing up the rear, I'm sure it was quite a race to behold. Finally, Mini dropped the rubber band and I pounced on it before Wanda could.

So why, you ask, am I walking chickens at all? Well, my husband kindly built me a chicken tractor, which is a movable coop. It's very well insulated against any kind of attack, whether from air, ground, or even underground.

Now, most chicken tractors don't have a bottom. But mine is fortified with a sturdy bottom panel, and although I move it around often, the girls can't really scratch in the dirt much. So when I'm outside or we see each other through the window, the girls give me sad "we want out" looks.

Because I hate seeing anything cooped up for very long (even an animal that generally spends its days in a place called a coop), I just give in and let them out for a little R and R in the backyard, in the flower beds, around the mulched trees, in the garden, and in general, anywhere they want to go.

Someone's got to stroll along with them. After all, our worthless cat doesn't do guard duty very well, nor does the next-door dog that visits us daily. And when you've only got four chickens, and they all have names and individual personalities and funny little quirks, how could you possibly even consider throwing them to the wolves, so to speak?

My husband says my chickens are spoiled. I'm not exactly sure why. It's not like I let them in the house to watch TV or anything. And right now I don't have time to fathom the mysteries of the male mind—I just caught a glimpse through the window of my four chickens, and they're in need of their morning walk. ☀

Our Stomping Grounds

Their ancestors farmed this land for more than a century and blazed a trail for them to follow.

BY REBECCA LANE *Tunkhannock, Pennsylvania*

Curious census takers around here have asked, "How many generations has your family lived on this property?" They notice something: Some families have been here a very long time My own family has been on this farm for five generations. I say it like it's something normal. Lanes have always been here. But when I stop to think about it, it's more awe-inspiring.

Since 1884, some person whose blood now runs in my veins has been here, was born here. And before 1884, an ancestor of mine, perhaps with a thick Yorkshire accent, made his way to this patch of ground, and began growing things and raising animals.

Maybe it was a bit like home, so he looked around and thought, *This is a good place*. He grew a life and raised a family. This patch of earth became our stomping grounds for well over a century.

The way it is with all families, there are stories told, "remember when" stories. About the time when my aunt, on her farm-bred Palomino, entered a horse race against fancy well-pedigreed steeds, and the lowly farm horse and its rider took the cup. Or when the tornado flew across the property under a green sky and toppled the dark woods. The police blocked all traffic past our house, but they didn't know about the back logging road through the woods. It became a thoroughfare to get by roadblocks to stranded families—because all farmers have roads to their fields.

There are smaller stories, too. Sunday dinners when all of the kids and grandkids gathered to eat and watch *Little House on the Prairie*, chase the dogs, feed the horses, or read in the shade of the giant weeping willow. I learned to ride horses here, just like my father and his father. I climbed into the hayloft of the barn built by my great-great-grandfather, and I jumped into piles of sweet-smelling hay set aside for horses.

We hiked into the woods behind the barn and picked blueberries, then froze them for the winter when knew we would be desperate for any remnant of the summer's sweetness. If we were really lucky, we might find some delicious wild strawberries no bigger than our thumbnails growing among the hay or timothy grass.

I never quite understood the magnitude of a heritage like this. To be able to go out and walk among the trees that quivered and whispered in the wind, and to understand that they were ours—as if a person could really own this, the rabbits, the bears, the deer, the trees and the beaver dams. Rather, I realized that like the animals and the rocks, I was simply a part of it. Our heritage, the forest and the farm were written into me, like the swirls of my fingerprints.

The ghosts of my ancestors do not haunt the property. There's no story about spooky figures or apparitions. But sometimes the work is hard. The fence is broken or the snow is deep, but the sap must be gathered and boiled. Or there's calves to be fed and sheep to be sheared.

When I walk in the woods past the ruins of one of the family's first houses on the property, possibly their first house in this country, I think of them making their go of it. Standing against the wind, the snow or the heat, planting the trees that I now pick apples from, or walking in the woods listening to the song of the forest.

I know I am not alone; I never will be. That's because my ancestors planted a family here, many generations ago, whose roots run deep. ☀

Clockwise from far left: Dad Rylan makes summer memories with the girls; little sister, Ruby, checks on the cattle; oldest daughter, Molly, is thrilled by the tomato harvest; fIve generations of Lanes have farmed this property.

CAPTURE THE BEAUTY AROUND YOU

SCRAPBOOK

We enjoyed field after field of color at this tulip farm in Washington's Skagit Valley.
Then we visited relatives and came home with bulbs for our own garden!
WENDY HARRISON *San Diego, California*

My backyard sanctuary welcomes many birds daily. One morning,
a breathtaking rose-breasted grosbeak caught my eye.
HERBERT FIELDS *West Lafayette, Indiana*

This old tractor—a Massey Harris, probably a 101 Senior—sits outside the entrance to California's Carrizo Plain National Monument. After years of driving by, we stopped when the conditions were perfect for a photo.
JODY LANGFORD *Templeton, California*

Spring is a wonderful time to see new life at Yellowstone National Park.
LAURIE GERBER *North Pole, Alaska*

These two friends pick "flowers" for their moms.
What mother doesn't love dandelions?
SUE JONKER *Byron Center, Michigan*

This photo of my daughter, Anna, brings back so
many memories of raising hens and chicks.
CRYSTAL HUNTER *Borger, Texas*

Our rooster watches over the farm and crows at the crack of dawn to let us know another day has begun.
CRYSTAL BLANK *Broomfield, Colorado*

My sister Becky took this shy guy's photo on her hobby ranch near Burgessville, Ontario.
BRENDA HANSEN *Clintonville, Wisconsin*

Digging in the dirt, climbing rock piles or playing baseball—my grandson Gabe loves being outside.
BECKY FARRELL *McCalla, Alabama*

It warms my heart to see my husband, Todd, passing the tradition of farming onto our grandson, Koltin.
JEWLY JENSEN *Tremonton, Utah*

Sunsets in the New Jersey Pinelands National Reserve cannot go unnoticed. It's good to get out in the bogs.
GARY MILLER *Tabernacle, New Jersey*

My 2-year-old son Blake loved running through the colorful flowers. He was delighted that spring has sprung!
NADIA CARBERRY *Germantown, Ohio*

While out planting corn, my husband called me to come and help fill the planter.
After a hard day's work, we were rewarded with a colorful sunset.
KATHERINE PLESSNER *Verona, North Dakota*

My son Colston fed sunflower seeds to this
cheerful feathered friend while softly stroking it.
MANDI WOOD *Cleveland, Georgia*

Jase, our Great Pyrenees puppy, loves to play
peekaboo with our kittens, Gerald (top) and Pig.
KIM DAHLHEIMER *Bethel, Ohio*

This calf was sick and little Jayden was taking such good care of her, hoping she would get better.
COURTNEY STIRLING *Meadville, Pennsylvania*

I followed this white-throated sparrow as it zipped gracefully from tree to tree.
LORI BRAMBLE *Cambridge, Maryland*

Our 2-year-old son, Bennett, likes putting his tractor to good use at our new home's construction site.
TAYLOR ROGERS *Wildwood, Florida*

My son, Joseph, was happy to tag along as my husband, Reuben, collected sap from maple trees.
MEGHAN SOMERO *New Ipswich, New Hampshire*

My boyfriend, Bill, is a fourth-generation dairy farmer. He loves cows and I love kittens! I spotted this young, playful pair near the milking barn.
REGINA HOLMES *Midland, Virginia*

This image of a friend of mine and his son shows how we pass our love of the land to the next generation.
MARK CLODFELTER *Bement, Illinois*

Nothing says spring more than new life! A young gray fox kit uses its senses to explore.
JIM KNOX *Wilton, Maine*

As they watch their daddy drive the tractor and plant crops, these boys want to be just like him.
NICOLE HACKLEY *Grygla, Minnesota*

We moved to a new home off the Blue Ridge Parkway, and country living is exciting for my son Zachary.
PATTIE TURNER *Floyd, Virginia*

I live on a huge bird migration path, and seeing red-eyed vireos is always a highlight for me.
DANIEL DRAUDT *Buffalo, New York*

When baby animals visited their dad's nursery, Siena and Justice were instantly enamored!
BETTY SMITH *Lynnwood, Washington*

We love living in a peaceful, rural area, surrounded by nature.
The vibrant colors in spring are simply breathtaking to behold.
BARBARA GOMEZ *Raeford, North Carolina*

FEEL THE LOVE OF COUNTRY

HEART ♥ SOUL

Surrounded by the Forest

They take time away from the city to teach their children to love nature.

BY BETH FARRIS *Indianapolis, Indiana*

I was born in Indianapolis and have lived here for most of my life. This is my family's hometown, and I take pride in showing my children where their grandparents grew up and went to school, the church where my grandmother taught Sunday school for 50 years, and all the other spots from our history that give us roots. I dearly love this place.

Through the years, however, I have watched developers remove more and more of our old trees. It saddens me deeply to watch the towering friends that I grew up admiring being cut down. I feel as though my city has become less beautiful.

My husband, Jeff, and I want our children to grow up surrounded by God's natural beauty. So we bought a cabin in Brown County between the town of Nashville and the city of Bloomington.

The cabin is near the T.C. Steele home, where the impressionist painter, of the famed Hoosier Group of artists, lived and worked during the early 1900s. Steele's widow, Selma, donated their 211-acre property to the Indiana Department of Conservation in 1945. Her generosity has preserved this piece of land for all of us.

I feel a real sense of peace here, where the country views are sweet to my eyes and my heart. It makes me happy that the kids are getting used to being surrounded by forest. At first they thought the trip was spooky, but they have slowly stopped feeling nervous about the long drive through the trees.

We go to the cabin once a month, just for a couple nights, and there is always something different and exciting happening. The kids get out of the car and immediately run around, exploring what's new.

One time enormous sycamore leaves, even bigger than the kids' heads, covered the ground, and they collected bouquets of them. On another visit in the spring, there were so many baby frogs everywhere that you really had to choose each step carefully. The kids, in seventh heaven, made little stables for them out of sticks.

And in November we arrived during the sandhill crane migration. Hundreds, maybe thousands, of the elegant

Beth and her daughter (top) visit T.C. Steele's art studio; the kids love to kayak (bottom).

Waterfront views captivate in every season. Continuing clockwise: Jeff and the kids explore Brown County State Park; the family cabin; nature provides plenty of entertainment.

Trips to our weekend cabin give me hope, both for the future of our state and for our children.

birds were out on the lake trilling their unique call, which sounds a bit like a bunch of children during recess.

Our cabin has an expansive view across Lake Monroe, a man-made reservoir covering more than 10,000 acres. We enjoy looking for tracks and other signs of wildlife around this watery sanctuary.

We can also see the Charles C. Deam Wilderness Area, Indiana's only federally protected wilderness area, from the cabin. The land was logged and settled in the 1800s, but the U.S. Forest Service began to rehabilitate and reforest the area during the Great Depression. It was officially designated a wilderness in 1982.

Trips to our weekend cabin give me hope, both for the future of our state and for our children. I had never seen a bald eagle in the wild until a couple of years ago. My kids saw one from our boat on our first visit here.

Connecting with nature teaches me that with careful and thoughtful choices, this landscape, God's marvelous creation, can still be restored, preserved and protected for future generations. ☀

Life Lessons from Papaw

His grandfather taught that actions speak louder than words.

BY JEFF WALKER *Athens, Tennessee*

Wearing his signature hat, Jeff's grandfather Johnie did an honest day's work, whether watering corn (far left) or mowing hay (below). Jeff with Mamaw Rose Lee and Papaw (left).

On Feb. 22, 1916, my hero was born. It would be some 55 years later that I came along and met my grandfather Johnie Hennessee. I called him Papaw.

I can't remember a time when I was not around Papaw. Before I started elementary school, we had bonded, and I learned a lot of life's lessons from him.

He bought me my first calf when I was 4, and I raised it on a bottle. **Lesson No. 1: Responsibility builds character.**

I sold the calf back to him after about a year or so. He gave me a $100 bill and I bought a bicycle. **Lesson No. 2: Hard work brings reward.** Or should it be that huge profits like that can only come from grandfathers?

Once I was "working" with him building tobacco beds. He swung the hammer and hit his shin. As he hopped around in pain, I explained that I once had hit myself with a hammer and didn't even cry. I was still only 4 years old. **Lesson No. 3: Someone is always watching to see how you react to what life hands you.** Or should it be only offer advice when someone asks?

Once we spent the better half of a day taking a man around town to get parts to fix his truck, which had broken down on the side of the road. We just stopped to see if we could help, and it turns out we could. **Lesson No. 4: There is always someone who needs help, and we should be looking for them.**

Once he bought a bull from a man and then decided he didn't want it. So he sold it at the stock barn and doubled his money. He returned to the man's house and split the profit. Papaw told him if he had known the bull was worth more, he would have paid more. **Lesson No. 5: Conduct business with the highest level of integrity.** And oh yeah—a clear conscience sleeps well at night.

My hero took a terrible blow in the fall of 1999. A stroke left him weak and unable to speak. For about seven years we watched him as he drew closer and closer to the end. His life on earth ended in the early morning hours of April 1, 2007.

Because Papaw had no way to verbally communicate, I foolishly thought the lessons would stop. But then I realized he had never spoken any of his lessons. Papaw taught them to me by example, carefully living his heroic life in the watchful eyes of his grandson. He had never

But then I realized he had never spoken any of his lessons. Papaw taught them to me by example...

told me to be honest, to treat others fairly, to pray each day, or to live a life with God in control. He simply did those things.

And so, in the weakest time of his life, he taught me the most important lesson: Actions speak louder than words.

It's been more than a decade since my grandfather's death. I think about him often, and about the time we spent together. He was an ordinary man who took on extraordinary powers simply by living his good life in full view of those around him.

Upon his death, Papaw left behind a small farm, a small bank account, and a huge legacy of honesty, integrity and love. ☀

Stirring Memories

Her mother's legacy lives on through a set of bowls.

BY MARY JUDITH FINA *Chardon, Ohio*

In today's modern home, one of the biggest selling points seems to be a large kitchen. It's popular now to have cupboards galore, abundant countertops, an island and sufficient space for family and friends to mill around.

Not so in my mother's bustling, busy kitchen. No one milled around there—they just passed through with the same conversation openers: "What's for dinner?" or "When's dinner?"

We lived in an old farmhouse and the kitchen was the size of a stamp. My mother could pick up a pot of boiling pasta from the stove, turn around, take two steps and drain the water in the sink. Her tools were right at hand.

Of all of them, my mom's mixing bowls have the most meaning to me.

She had a set of four stainless steel bowls that she used every day. I'm not sure how she got them—perhaps they were a gift from my father or grandmother—but I know they first appeared during the 1960s.

The bowls range in size from small to large. Three of them had a small ring attached to the rim, something she could slip a finger through for a better grip while she was stirring or pouring.

She used her beloved bowls to create so many special recipes. She made double batches of cookie dough in the largest one and Jell-O in the smallest; sometimes she'd keep chicken soup in the refrigerator in a bowl to chill until the fat rose to the top. I rarely remember seeing those bowls empty, and I rarely saw my mother idle.

It would be impossible to calculate the pounds of flour used in her kitchen over all those years. She produced countless loaves of bread, plus pies, cookies, cakes and banana cupcakes with mocha frosting. Christmas and Easter always meant delicious Slovenian *potica*, a sweet bread, from her side of the family, and the Italian cookies filled with chocolate and dried fruit of my dad's heritage.

Those bowls served her well for nearly three decades. These days the special bowls adorn my kitchen, with the small rings still attached, and I use them from time to time to make biscuits, scones and cheesecakes. When I slip my finger through those rings, I like to think my hand is still holding hers. ☀

Mary Rose Fina, author Mary Judith Fina's mother, was known for her presence in the kitchen.

Bird lovers build nesting boxes like this one (inset) to encourage bluebirds to visit.

As the Bluebird Flies

Sometimes the best-laid garden plans encourage creative pranks.

BY MARCELLA MILLER *East Tawas, Michigan*

The first of April, and it still was cold. Icy snow tried its best to melt. And the phrase "cabin fever" came to mind.

This, my friends, is what ailed a Kentucky girl living in the beautiful state of Michigan with its four seasons. It just doesn't seem balanced when winter seems to outlast the others.

But April is also when dear neighbors generously pass along their seed and plant catalogs to keep this old brain of mine turning.

I began planning for a new garden, but it wouldn't work in such a small yard unless my garden hutch was moved to the opposite side. This shed was handcrafted of cedar. My husband and I had hauled it here on the bed of a truck in weather much worse than this.

Channeling the strength and spirit of the Little Engine That Could (and with a couple of long boards and strong will) we moved the hutch across the melting snow. It took us three days.

Now my gardening plan could grow! The spot where my hutch once stood would be a perfect hummingbird and butterfly area. Research, reading and replanting became my new focus.

Another mostly shaded area caught my eye because it would be perfect for naturalistic planting. I would try my luck with herbs in the old vegetable garden. Their presence should wake up the whole yard.

And I found a new home for the bluebird house I bought when we moved here five years ago.

From sunup to sundown, we removed tree roots, transplanted perennials, and amended and added new soil. The work was difficult but I really loved how it all came together.

Then early one morning as I rushed among the three gardens like a crazy woman, my husband said he had just seen a bluebird fly into the bluebird house. I stopped at a distance: "I see it! I see it!" Excited, I tried to keep calm so it wouldn't fly away.

"I can't believe it," I said. "The bluebird is looking right at me!"

My husband chuckled, then confessed that it had been in there for days. He had put an old ceramic bluebird in my birdhouse.

A prank like this will either make a lady crazier or give her a good laugh. I chose the latter.

Right now a family of hummingbirds and three monarch butterflies are welcome guests in my garden. Every day brings a new surprise as I relax surrounded by God's beauty. And I know that someday I will finally get that bluebird! ☀

Dinnertime with Family

They relish every moment together in a life they love.

BY SUSAN GROVE *Gettysburg, Pennsylvania*

My husband, Craig, is a farm laborer, and I am so proud of him and his work.

I come from a family who has farmed the land for several generations, so marrying someone who does farmwork was almost second nature to me. I fit right in to the farming lifestyle of rural Pennsylvania.

Like so many farmers, Craig works long days during planting and harvesting. And like many farm wives, it's not unusual for me to get a request to bring some dinner to him in the field. There's simply no time for him to stop working and come home for a meal.

Our dog Ziva loves these trips. She not only goes for a beloved car ride, but also spends time with Craig. ☀

Craig and farm dog Ziva share some quality time planting corn in the spring.

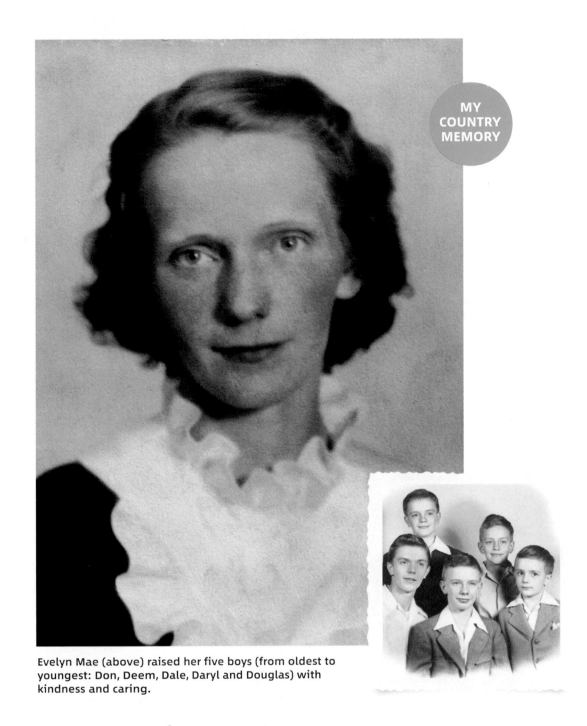

Evelyn Mae (above) raised her five boys (from oldest to youngest: Don, Deem, Dale, Daryl and Douglas) with kindness and caring.

Grit and Grace

His mother was the heart and soul of the family.

BY DALE DICKSON *Eugene, Oregon*

No matter how mischievous her five rowdy boys were, my mother, Evelyn Mae, nurtured us with unconditional love and patience. It wasn't easy during the Great Depression. Dad was always working, and that left Mother to raise us. There were times when she didn't have enough money to buy a 3-cent stamp, but she still put a decent meal on the table. We grew most of our food, and Mother canned vegetables and sewed clothing for us out of flour sacks.

She was a rock and a saint who gave us a set of values to live by. She was our mother, comforter, teacher and nurse—a true example of grace. Her kindness still lingers with me. ☀

Zesty Sugar Snap Peas

TAKES: 15 min. • **MAKES:** 4 servings

- 1 lb. fresh or frozen sugar snap peas
- ½ cup water
- 1 Tbsp. butter
- 1 garlic clove, minced
- ¾ tsp. lemon-pepper seasoning
- ¼ tsp. salt

In a skillet, bring peas and water to a boil. Reduce heat. Cover and cook until tender, 6-7 minutes. Drain. Add the remaining ingredients. Cook and stir until well-coated, 2-3 minutes.

¾ **cup:** 74 cal., 3g fat (2g sat. fat), 8mg chol., 267mg sod., 8g carb. (4g sugars, 3g fiber), 4g pro.
Diabetic exchanges: 1 vegetable, ½ fat.

Strawberry-Rhubarb Flip Cake

PREP: 20 min. · **BAKE:** 40 min. + cooling · **MAKES:** 12 servings

- 1 cup packed brown sugar
- 3 Tbsp. quick-cooking tapioca
- 6 cups sliced fresh or frozen rhubarb, thawed
- 3 cups sliced fresh or frozen strawberries, thawed
- ½ cup butter, softened
- 1 cup sugar
- 2 large eggs, room temperature
- 1 tsp. vanilla extract
- 2 cups all-purpose flour
- 2½ tsp. baking powder
- ¼ tsp. salt
- 1 cup 2% milk
  Sweetened whipped cream or vanilla ice cream, optional

1. Preheat oven to 350°. In a large bowl, mix brown sugar and tapioca. Add rhubarb and strawberries; toss to coat. Let stand 15 minutes.

2. Meanwhile, in a large bowl, cream the butter and sugar until light and fluffy. Add 1 egg at a time, beating well after each addition. Beat in vanilla. In another bowl, whisk flour, baking powder and salt; add to creamed mixture alternately with the milk, beating well after each addition.

3. Transfer rhubarb mixture to a greased 13x9-in. baking dish; pour batter over top. Bake 40-45 minutes or until a toothpick inserted in the center comes out clean. Cool completely in pan on a wire rack. Invert each piece onto a serving plate. If desired, serve with whipped cream or ice cream.

NOTE If using frozen rhubarb, measure rhubarb while still frozen, then thaw completely. Drain in a colander, but do not press liquid out.

1 piece: 338 cal., 9g fat (5g sat. fat), 53mg chol., 223mg sod., 60g carb. (38g sugars, 2g fiber), 5g pro.

Strawberry-Feta Tossed Salad

TAKES: 10 min. · **MAKES:** 6 servings

- 6 cups torn mixed salad greens
- 2 cups fresh strawberries, sliced
- 1 pkg. (4 oz.) crumbled feta cheese
- ¼ cup sunflower kernels
  Balsamic vinaigrette

Place the first 4 ingredients in a large bowl. To serve, drizzle with vinaigrette; toss to combine.

1 cup: 103 cal., 6g fat (2g sat. fat), 10mg chol., 259mg sod., 8g carb. (3g sugars, 3g fiber), 6g pro.

Farmers Breakfast

TAKES: 20 min. · **MAKES:** 4 servings

- 6 bacon strips, diced
- 2 Tbsp. diced onion
- 3 medium potatoes, cooked and cubed
- 6 large eggs, beaten
   Salt and pepper to taste
- ½ cup shredded cheddar cheese

1. In a cast-iron or other heavy skillet, cook bacon until crisp. Remove to paper towels to drain. In the drippings, saute onion and potatoes until potatoes are browned, about 5 minutes. Push potato mixture from center to sides of pan. Pour eggs into center; cook and stir gently until eggs are set and cooked to desired doneness. Stir to combine eggs and potato mixture.
2. Season with salt and pepper. Sprinkle with cheese and bacon; let stand until cheese melts.

1 serving: 464 cal., 29g fat (11g sat. fat), 321mg chol., 487mg sod., 30g carb. (2g sugars, 3g fiber), 21g pro.

Rise & Shine Parfait

TAKES: 15 min. · **MAKES:** 4 servings

- 4 cups fat-free vanilla yogurt
- 2 medium peaches, chopped
- 2 cups fresh blackberries
- ½ cup granola without raisins or Kashi Go Lean Crunch cereal

Layer half of the yogurt, peaches, blackberries and granola into 4 parfait glasses. Repeat layers.

1 parfait: 259 cal., 3g fat (0 sat. fat), 7mg chol., 6mg sod., 48g carb. (27g sugars, 7g fiber), 13g pro.

Sour Cream & Cheddar Biscuits

PREP: 25 min. • **BAKE:** 15 min.
MAKES: 1½ dozen

- 2½ cups all-purpose flour
- 3 tsp. baking powder
- 2 tsp. sugar
- 1 tsp. garlic powder
- ½ tsp. cream of tartar
- ¼ tsp. salt
- ¼ tsp. cayenne pepper
- ½ cup cold butter, cubed
- 1½ cups shredded cheddar cheese
- ¾ cup 2% milk
- ½ cup sour cream

TOPPING
- 6 Tbsp. butter, melted
- 1½ tsp. garlic powder
- 1 tsp. minced fresh parsley

1. Preheat oven to 450°. In a large bowl, whisk first 7 ingredients. Cut in cold butter until the mixture resembles coarse crumbs; stir in cheese. Add milk and sour cream; stir just until moistened.
2. Drop by ¼ cupfuls 2 in. apart onto greased baking sheets. Mix topping ingredients; brush over tops. Bake 12-15 minutes or until light brown. Serve warm.

1 biscuit: 206 cal., 14g fat (8g sat. fat), 36mg chol., 256mg sod., 15g carb. (2g sugars, 1g fiber), 5g pro.

Chard with Bacon-Citrus Sauce

TAKES: 25 min. · **MAKES:** 6 servings

- ½ **lb. thick-sliced peppered bacon strips**
- 2 **lbs. rainbow Swiss chard, chopped**
- 1 **cup orange juice**
- 2 **Tbsp. butter**
- 4 **tsp. grated orange zest**
- ⅛ **tsp. salt**
- ⅛ **tsp. pepper**

1. In a large cast-iron or other heavy skillet, cook bacon over medium heat until crisp; drain on paper towels. Discard all but 1 Tbsp. of drippings. Cut bacon into small pieces.
2. Add Swiss chard to drippings; cook and stir just until wilted, 5-6 minutes. Add the remaining ingredients; cook 1-2 minutes, stirring occasionally. Top with bacon.

½ **cup:** 162 cal., 11g fat (5g sat. fat), 22mg chol., 655mg sod., 10g carb. (5g sugars, 3g fiber), 7g pro.

Ultimate Scalloped Potatoes

PREP: 20 min. + cooling • **BAKE:** 1 hour • **MAKES:** 6 servings

- 1 tsp. butter, softened
- 1 cup heavy whipping cream
- ⅓ cup whole milk
- 1 tsp. salt
- ½ tsp. pepper
- 2 garlic cloves, crushed
- 6 medium potatoes
- 1 cup shredded Swiss cheese
- ¼ cup shredded Parmesan cheese

1. Grease a shallow 13x9-in. baking dish with the butter; set aside. In a small saucepan, combine the cream, milk, salt, pepper and garlic. Cook just until bubbles begin to form around sides of pan. Remove from the heat; cool for 10 minutes.

2. Peel and thinly slice the potatoes; pat dry with paper towels. Layer half of the potatoes in prepared baking dish; top with half of the cream mixture and half of the cheeses. Repeat layers.

3. Bake, covered, at 350° for 40 minutes. Uncover and continue baking until potatoes are tender, 20-25 minutes longer. Let stand for 5-10 minutes before serving.

1 serving: 402 cal., 22g fat (14g sat. fat), 77mg chol., 538mg sod., 41g carb. (6g sugars, 3g fiber), 12g pro.

Ham Pasta Toss

TAKES: 25 min. • **MAKES:** 6 servings

- 12 oz. uncooked whole wheat spaghetti
- 3 Tbsp. butter
- 2 cups shredded or cubed fully cooked ham
- 2 garlic cloves, minced
- 3 cups frozen peas (about 12 oz.), thawed
- 2 Tbsp. minced fresh parsley
- ¼ cup grated Parmesan cheese

1. Cook spaghetti according to package directions; drain. Meanwhile, in a large skillet, heat butter over medium heat. Add ham; cook and stir 2-4 minutes or until browned. Add garlic; cook 1 minute longer.

2. Stir in spaghetti, peas and parsley; heat through. Sprinkle with cheese; toss to combine.

1⅓ cups: 374 cal., 10g fat (5g sat. fat), 46mg chol., 738mg sod., 52g carb. (3g sugars, 10g fiber), 23g pro.

HANDCRAFTED WITH LOVE

Spring Door Decor

Combine April showers and
May flowers with this fresh
front-door welcome.

WHAT YOU'LL NEED
- Vintage umbrella
- Floral picks
- Ribbon

DIRECTIONS
1. Unsnap umbrella closure. Arrange
   floral picks into bouquet, placing
   stems inside inverted umbrella.
2. Close umbrella and fasten snap
   to secure bouquet.
3. Tie ribbon around umbrella
   to conceal closure.

Plant Markers

Recall what's planted where with these easy-to-make garden tags.

WHAT YOU'LL NEED

- Plastic wrap
- Masking tape
- Air-drying clay
- Rag
- Bamboo or barbecue skewer
- Alphabet stamp set
- Decorative twine

DIRECTIONS

1. Cover a surface with plastic wrap and tape down edges.
2. Tear off a small amount of the clay and roll it into a ¾-in.-diameter ball.
3. Flatten ball on plastic into an even, smooth round disk about ⅛ in. thick. (For longer plant names, make the disk into more of an oval shape.) If the clay starts to dry out and small cracks form around the edges of disks, use a damp rag to gently smooth them over.
4. Use a bamboo skewer to make a hole about ⅓ in. from the top edge of the disk.
5. Press the plant name into the clay disk using alphabet stamps. Begin with middle letters and work outward.
6. Allow the clay to air-dry overnight. Thread decorative twine through the hole.
7. Tie the label to a plant pot, a garden stake or even to the stem of a plant itself.

Recipe Card Wall Hanging

Cook up a rustic piece of artwork to display a cherished family memento.

WHAT YOU'LL NEED

- Reclaimed wood planks
- Wood strips
- Recipe card
- Decoupage glue
- Twine
- Finish nailer
- Photocopier
- Paintbrush
- Drill

DIRECTIONS

1. Arrange reclaimed wood planks to create a rectangular base. Arrange the wood strips on the back of the planks, perpendicular to the seams between the planks. Nail strips to planks, securing them in place.
2. Enlarge recipe card on a color copier, choosing a size slightly smaller than base dimensions.
3. Apply decoupage glue on back of print and press it into place on wood. Brush another layer of glue over entire front to seal it. Dry thoroughly.
4. Drill holes in upper corners of wood base and thread twine through holes, knotting ends to secure.

The Curtis Island Lighthouse, built in
1836, stands at the entrance to Camden
Harbor in Maine.
PHOTO BY PAUL REZENDES

Summer

THE GOOD LIFE

Sharing My Bliss

Surrounded by the beauty and blessings of her family's farm, she feels on top of the world.

BY SARAH J. MARSH *Bliss, New York*

Our farm sits on the highest elevation point of Wyoming County in western New York. From a distance, you can distinguish it by the silo and even taller pine tree.

Up here, we enjoy the sunrises, sunsets, rainbows, a night sky full of stars, and once even the aurora borealis! On a clear day we can see to the farthest hill on the horizon about 30 miles away, with a bit of farm country, a few houses, and woods in between. Some mornings we can see a fog bank coming off the Genesee River in the Letchworth State Park gorge.

While I was growing up, this was a true family farm. My dad milked about 35 Holstein cows, and we had heifers, calves, chickens, pigs (once!), horses (for a while), cats, bunnies, one pet pigeon, and the best dog-friend ever, Dixie. We also grew hay, oats and corn.

My big brother, Bill, raised some pheasants for 4-H. He and I also showed heifers for many years at the Wyoming County Fair. I much preferred doing barn chores over any house chores, as my mom will tell you. Some things never change!

My mom and dad, Christine and Stanley, still live

Summer brings pleasant weather to the Marsh family farm, which sits at the peak of a hill.

Clockwise from top left: Niece Maggie cuddles a kid; nephew Noah helps Aunt Sarah on the hay wagon; hollyhocks in bloom; goats follow Sarah.

on the farm. They have always been avidly involved in our small community, with Dad serving on the town board and Mom staying active in the church and being a friendly neighbor. We held Halloween hayrides for many years, taking all the kids from our road trick-or-treating.

I moved away for a while but returned about four years ago, frequently visiting home to take walks up to the stress-free fields at the top of our hill and to seek the serenity of silence on starry nights. Now I live about a half-hour away and work as a teacher. I come over to the farm at least once a week.

When my dad retired from dairy farming he raised beef for many years and also tried beekeeping. He and I recently delved into the Boer meat-goat business.

Bill's family also lives nearby. My nieces and nephew

I feel closest to my family when we work together.

like to help out around the farm, and two of the children had blue-ribbon goat showings at the fair last summer.

If I had to describe our farm in one word, it would be windy. My big brother is the only reason I did not blow away on many a winter morning waiting for the bus! Deep snow is another fact of life up here because of the elevation. Mom and Dad often won't leave the house because of a blizzard.

I feel closest to my family when we work together, whether we're weeding in the garden, doing some construction projects, chopping wood or caring for the animals.

It's fun when family or friends help us at the farm. I really love sharing our bliss, especially in summer. There's nothing like the warm days of haying season. We rake, bale, haul wagons and go in the haymow. Carrying two bales is still the best workout I get!

The land and our life here has given us so many gifts: milk, beef, fruits and vegetables, maple syrup, eggs, spectacular views, wildlife sightings, work ethic and pride. I have traveled to 50 states and other countries, and there's no place that I love more than these hills. ☀

The Transplant

A former city girl learned to embrace her new country life.

BY CYNTHIA PAPPAS *Springfield, Oregon*

I left behind my Southern California valley girl days in 1980 to attend graduate school in Oregon. After earning my master's degree, I found a job with a regional planning agency working on a long-range urbanization plan.

My job involved contentious meetings with the public and various officials. But during one meeting, I noticed a really cute commissioner who asked a lot of seriously smart questions. Smart always works on me. After a little sleuthing, I found out his name was George and that he wasn't married.

As it turns out, he'd been equally impressed by my smart answers and had done some sleuthing of his own. George asked me out and we hit it off, marrying in 1988. Along with my new husband, I gained two stepsons, a farm, two dogs, a commercial raspberry operation and a whole new education.

I had absolutely no qualms about moving to a 66-acre spread near the Willamette Valley in Oregon—after all, what could be complicated about taking care of a barn, a shop and a huge farmhouse? Since I grew up in Los Angeles and had mastered things like rush-hour traffic on the 405 freeway and finding a parking spot at the mall, I figured I could handle anything. This attitude did not serve me well on the farm.

One day while playing a farming board game with George and the boys, I tested my newfound knowledge.

"I just lost my wheat field."

"No, Cindy, that's your second cutting of hay you just lost," Nat, the oldest, quickly informed me.

"Wheat...hay...what's the difference?" I quipped, quickly passing the dice to their father to distract them. This transplant needed more time to develop roots.

When I moved onto the farm in early July, it was the height of raspberry season—a great time for me to learn a lot, and fast. The phone rang constantly, with folks calling to ask if we had "U-pick," which was a new term to this city girl. Farmers around here offer U-pick raspberries, blueberries, pumpkins, apples, pears, cherries and strawberries. You could spend the entire summer U-picking.

Another big lesson came one night when one of our neighbor's cows got out. Returning home from a city council meeting, I almost drove into the cow on our half-mile gravel driveway. After I maneuvered my car around

Cynthia grew up in Los Angeles, moving to an Oregon farm after she married George.

the cow, I noticed my husband hanging his head out of our second-story bedroom window.

"Hey hon," he called down. "Since you still have your shoes on, could you get that cow back into the neighbor's pasture? She's been bellowing and I know she's thirsty."

Though I wondered how my husband could possibly know the cow was thirsty, I hopped out of the car, still in my heels and a suit, and walked slowly toward the loudly mooing cow.

"Shoo. Yaw. Go on," I said firmly. These words usually make animals move, but nothing worked.

"Grab a stick and hit it on the butt!" George yelled between fits of laughter. I grabbed a branch but was not about to get close enough to the cow to reach her fanny, so I whacked the stick on the ground and repeated my verbal prodding. The cow never even looked up.

From top: Cynthia has come to love all types of animals since embracing the country life; the Pappas family grows tomatoes and raspberries, along with other produce.

The standoff finally ended when George put on his boots and came outside. His one strong whack and a loud "Yaw!" sent the cow back into the neighbor's pasture.

Living on this farm, I've learned to share my life with a lot more than just wandering cows. We have a bee colony living under the eaves, and the dogs catch gophers. I disagree with John Denver's portrayal of farm life as "kinda laid back"—we must constantly and vigilantly search for moles in the garden, mice in the laundry room and starlings that accidentally come down the chimney into the living room. (The latter required me to grab my stepson's butterfly net to catch and release the bird outdoors.) As a fifth-generation farmer, my husband takes it all in stride while I continue to learn and grow.

Mastering the bewildering array of farm equipment remains a work in progress. When I am at wits' end, I remind George there is a reason these machines are referred to as implements of husbandry.

Living here has given me a sense of neighborliness I couldn't have imagined in Los Angeles. We exchange zucchini for sunflower bouquets, salsa for use of the extension ladder. We help each other cut and stack hay in late June. When the power goes out, whoever has a generator invites the others over to watch TV in a warm house. We share the rhythm of the seasons and feel extraordinarily blessed to live along the McKenzie River.

This transplant has grown deep roots. I thrive now on being in touch with the land, and feel myself blooming from the love of this new, extended family. ☀

There's lots to love about life in Oregon, including the beauty of the outdoors.

Falling in Love with Nature

Exploring gives this couple special experiences together.

BY SHELBY KISGEN *Powell, Wyoming*

Hiking is one of the best ways to see the countryside. From an evening amble around the cow pasture to a three-day backpacking trip into the mountains, walking grounds me.

Time spent in nature reminds me of simple joys and healthy living. The scenes our eyes absorb feed our souls. There is nothing like appreciating the glory of God's creation. Exploring improves our lives, bonds us with our adventure partners, and helps us to focus on the bigger picture—the world around us.

My husband, Cody, snapped this photo of me in the Bighorn Mountain range near Sheridan, Wyoming. It was July 2016, during our annual anniversary backpacking trip. We celebrate every year together by venturing to new mountain ranges. ☀

Shelby hikes through the Bighorn Mountains on an anniversary trip with her husband, Cody.

Our Americana House

She finished her husband's project in his memory.

BY BENITA WOODARD *Grants Pass, Oregon*

My husband, Richard, was a true patriot. We were married 49 years, and when he passed away six years ago, I finished a tiny house that he had begun to build. I call it the Americana House to honor Richard's love for this country.

Our neighbor, Pete, helped me finish it. We didn't have any plans to follow, but as ideas occurred to me, Pete made them happen. He added a picket fence, vaulted ceiling, porch and cupola. Painting the fence white inspired me to do the trim and decor in a patriotic red, white and blue.

This tiny house has brought me a lot of joy. I like to relax on the front porch when I'm working in my flower beds, and friends and neighbors often come over to visit. It takes us all back to our childhoods.

I had wished for this house as a child. Now I have it, and I know Richard would be proud. ☀

Where We Belong

Their roots run deep in these scenic hills, surrounded by farmland and flowers.

BY CANDY THOMPSON *Kingwood, West Virginia*

It is so nice to wake up in the morning, get a cup of coffee and sit out on the front porch. Our alarm clock is the birds, singing at the break of day. My husband, Larry, and I have lovely views of a country barn, a field of cows and a row of hills.

Larry grew up next door to where we live now. He decided a long time ago to build a home here because, "We have a wonderful view of the mountains—and fresh country air."

I also grew up in Preston County, just outside of where we live in Kingwood. As you drive around on our country roads, you can see rolling hills and forest everywhere, with farmland and livestock all around.

Kingwood is a small town. You can take a leisurely walk and look at the wooden buildings that date back to the 1800s. It has changed very little in the last 100 years. Most of the streets were built in the 1930s by the WPA (Works Progress Administration).

Every time we go to town, we see someone we grew up with or are related to. Around here when you make a friend, you are friends for life. Larry can ride his John Deere tractor down the road on a Sunday afternoon and share a friendly wave with the neighbors. We all know

and call each other by our first names.

I enjoy photography, and we live in a great place to capture scenic Appalachian views. Across the road from our front yard is the old barn, which Larry says has been there as long as he can remember. I have taken photos of it throughout the changing seasons. The mountains behind the barn add to the already peaceful scenery. It's like looking at a postcard, all year-round.

From early spring until late autumn, cows come to graze in the farm field. After a nice rain shower you can hear the soothing sound of a creek flowing.

Behind our home, there's a trail where train tracks used to be. It's a quiet place to forage for natural herbs and wild ramps.

On summer nights, frogs chirp and lightning bugs glow. Unless it is really cloudy, a blanket of stars covers the sky, with the moon shining so brightly.

Many years ago, Larry and his mom planted apple trees in our yard. We continued this tradition by planting a tree for each of our grandchildren—a pear tree for Alec, a crabapple tree for Jacob and cherry tree for Tyler. As the trees grow, our grandchildren will learn how important they are to the health of our environment.

Candy and Larry (top) planted butterfly-friendly flower beds (above). Left: Hyacinths and tulips bloom in Kingwood.

In the springtime apple and pear blossoms provide the bees with nectar and the bees, in turn, pollinate them. When the fruit is ripe, there is nothing like a slice of homemade apple pie, apple dumplings or pear muffins. We have raspberry and blackberry bushes, too. We freeze most of our berries so we can bake cobblers throughout winter. Recently we planted blueberries, and we can't wait for the fruit.

There is always something in bloom during spring, summer and autumn. I tease Larry about the flower beds, saying he didn't even know what a flower bed was until I moved in!

In spring, tulips and hyacinths always come in first. Then we see lilies and irises of all colors, followed by coneflowers, black-eyed Susans and daisies. Clematis vines grow on the side of the house. Butterfly bushes, rose of Sharon shrubs and rhododendrons bloom all around the property.

My flowers provide a natural feeding habitat for the insects and butterflies. Monarchs, great spangled fritillaries, swallowtails and hummingbird moths are quite common here.

We plant a garden every year with lettuce, tomatoes, carrots, green beans, squash, cucumbers and onions. Sometimes the bunnies pay a visit to the garden. That's OK; we plant extra for them. The bunnies also nibble on the clover that grows among the grass.

Birdbaths provide clean water. We put out feeders year-round for birds and squirrels, and we also have several birdhouses.

The birds also build nests in the evergreen hedge that runs along one side of the yard. In the early summer, you can hear nestlings chirping away while their parents scurry about gathering food.

While sitting out on our back porch swing, Larry and I like to watch the hummingbirds come up to drink our sugar water. Occasionally, one will stop and rest a bit on the flowerpots.

Sometimes, we see some turkeys or deer darting in and out of the woods. At night the deer come into our yard to eat the fallen apples and leftover vegetables that we put in a pile.

I've always been a country girl. This land is where our roots are. And this is the place that Larry and I will always call home. ☀

It's like looking at a postcard, all year-round.

From top: Candy loves driving along the back roads of Preston County, spring apple blossoms and local bird-watching.

The Farm Brings Us Together

Every year their family reunites on the land where their story began.

BY DOLORES BODENSCHATZ *North Canton, Ohio*

The Great Depression couldn't dampen the love of my parents, John and Jenny Wirfel, who were married on Oct. 3, 1933. But their move to a farm in the Allegheny Mountains in Cambria Township, Pennsylvania, was a challenge, to say the least.

The place had been vacated for years and was very run-down. Dad said he could count the stars while milking the cow. Mum chimed in that the house looked worse than the barn.

Back in the 1920s and '30s, when relatives got together to work (or play), they called the occasion a frolic. Mum and Dad worked to repair the barn, house and fences during a frolic with their brothers' and sisters' aid.

The men did the labor while the women brought order to the house and provided food for a big feast at noon and again when work was finished for the day.

Jenny and John Wirfel (left) grew a legacy of love. Their family gathers for reunions every summer (top).

My dad's family was typically industrious, but my mum's side loved to laugh, sing, joke and have a good time, so my parents made a great combination.

They moved onto the farm in May of 1934 and raised seven sons and three daughters. We had cows, pigs, chickens, a large garden and several varieties of fruit trees. Not one of us kids ever went hungry.

In 1952, Mum and Dad decided to build an addition to the house which included a bathroom with a flush toilet.

Dolores' brother Duck (inset) owns the family farm (above), where 10 kids grew up and put down roots.

Dolores says several of her family members like quilting, so it seemed appropriate for her sisters to paint a quilt square on the shed door.

Gone was the Saturday night galvanized bathtub. Now there was no more brushing snow off the outhouse seat before I sat down.

Sadly, both Mum and Dad have passed, but for over 40 years the younger generations have carried on their tradition of having family reunions at the farm. We can't wait for the annual gathering.

We now number more than 200 family members, including me, my husband, Dennis, our five living children, 18 grandchildren and two great-grandchildren. Usually we have around 160 people in attendance. I'm constantly amazed that the second and third cousins know and love each other, even though we are scattered across 10 different states.

Smartphones help keep everyone in touch even though we may only see each other once a year. So to keep track of whose children are whose, each sibling is assigned a different color to wear.

The family reunion has grown to include three days of laughter and fun, food, the occasional barn dance with a live band, food, card games, ballgames and more food. The local priest graciously comes to the farm to celebrate Mass for us under a rented tent on Saturday.

My bachelor brother Duck (Don) owns the 150-year-old farm. He is physically unable to work the land, so a neighbor farmer plants hay and corn—and always mows the hay for our makeshift softball field.

We all do our part to care for the property. My own family goes back several times a year to maintain the buildings and do any necessary upkeep. Four other siblings who live nearby also help. We hold a workday every year. Several family members like quilting, so it seemed appropriate for my sisters to paint a quilt square on the shed door.

I've heard it said that after the parents are gone, the reunions fall apart. That hasn't happened to our family, thank God. We will be forever grateful to Mum and Dad for their courage to settle on a run-down farm in Pennsylvania and watch their love bloom. ☀

CAPTURE THE BEAUTY AROUND YOU

SCRAPBOOK

My great-granddaughter Harper Ruth is fast becoming a country girl as she gets her first taste of watermelon.
She loves it, not only because it's so yummy, but also because it matches her outfit!
RUTH HARRIS *Austin, Texas*

Talk about inspiring! My beloved granddaughter Kristen Wineinger took this photo of a patriotic barn in Vernon, New Jersey, just as the sun was starting to set.
META STAVRAND *Highland Lakes, New Jersey*

We enjoyed this scene on one of the farms during our tour of the Amish community in Harmony, Minnesota.
KAREN BERG *Elk River, Minnesota*

While at a local park, I noticed a lot of thistle. The goldfinches went crazy over the food source.
KALLEY COOK *Lenoir City, Tennessee*

My daughter Emily had a laugh when our friend's baby goat nibbled on her neck during a visit.
HILLARY SPHULER *Kalispell, Montana*

We've bottle-fed our favorite Jersey steer since he was a few days old, and he and our youngest farmer (3 years old in this picture) truly love each other. Raising children on a farm is a blessing.
KASEY HENDRICK *Bowling Green, Kentucky*

Royal and magnificent are spot-on descriptions for the regal fritillary.
This one sipped nectar from a butterfly weed in my backyard.
GAIL HUDDLE *McPherson, Kansas*

My grandma, Deloris Zastrow, led my kids, Bailey, Case and Corban, down the street in their own parade!
STEPHANIE ARNDT *Mayville, Wisconsin*

Kirk Otto, whose farm I help out on, got this photo of my daughter Brynnleigh on a combine ride.
MICHAEL GASPER *New Lothrop, Michigan*

I love seeing all the homemade signs in Lancaster County, Pennsylvania, during the summer.
CAROL NORWOOD *Myerstown, Pennsylvania*

An American flag decorates the Cilleyville Bog Bridge in Andover, New Hampshire. The structure is listed on the National Registry of Historic Places.
PHOTO BY PAUL REZENDES

A friend and I were out taking photos, and this friendly fella came right up to the fence and posed for us.
DANNY REDD *Galax, Virginia*

At the bridge, the younger children like to follow the weedy path underneath to fish in the shade.
REBECCA KOMPPA *Sebeka, Minnesota*

Summer means county fairs and fun for our grandkids, Madison (left) and her cousin, Maddy.
SUSAN TERRY *Battle Creek, Michigan*

This male rufous enjoyed a light shower in Astoria, Oregon. I love his bold attitude and bright colors.
TRISH NEVAN *Terrebonne, Oregon*

Watching the bears catch fish during the salmon run in Katmai National Park in Alaska is amazing.
GERALD P. RUNDE *Teutopolis, Illinois*

My sister took me to her friend's dairy farm, and Yari the cow stuck her head out to say hello!
TERRI HOBBS *Ridgeway, Ontario*

Our 2-year-old granddaughter, Annie, was filled with patriotic pride in Saugatuck, Michigan.
CARYN YOUNG *Crest Hill, Illinois*

Hume Lake in Sequoia National Park is special to me, as I spent many summers there. It's a perfect place to focus on nature and family.
BROOKE GERLACH *Palm Springs, California*

It was such a proud moment when my son Jack used his Farmall B
restoration project for the first time to put up hay.
ANDREA SCHNEIDER *Berger, Missouri*

Nature is beautiful and powerful, even when you least expect it.
KEVIN WILSON *Colorado Springs, Colorado*

When it poured one day the kids put on boots
and splashed in mud puddles.
LAURA ROSS *Ovalo, Texas*

You can see why my daughter Mikayla loves to go
work with her daddy on our third-generation dairy.
COURTNEY VANTOL *Ramona, California*

Our canna plants grew so tall last summer that we decided to take a family photo to capture the moment!
ANGIE CROW *Arnold, Nebraska*

When my husband bought a new tractor, our sons couldn't wait to line up for a group photo.
LYNDSIE CARLSON *Quimby, Iowa*

Ella, my 4-year-old daughter, is already patriotic. When our flag was tangled, she fixed it.
WENDI KNIGHT *Green Cove Springs, Florida*

Last Dollar Road is a gem in the mountains. Wildflower meadows
and ranches under a brilliant blue sky just blow me away.
DON PAGE *Salida, Colorado*

Ways of the Pioneers

Crossing the North Dakota prairie in a covered wagon
tested endurance and changed her life.

BY ANNA WESTERMAN *Sauk Centre, Minnesota*

From left: Lexie, Sierra, Katie, Anna and Naomi catch up during the noon stop for dinner.

Have you ever wanted to travel like a pioneer, crossing the open prairie in wagons with only the jingle of horses' harnesses and the joyful sounds of laughter to entertain you?

Well, I have. Seven years ago, my sister, Grace, our cousin Morgan and I saddled up and joined the Fort Seward Wagon Train. This annual camping journey starts in mid- to late June and re-creates the pioneers' journey west across North Dakota in the 1800s.

It starts at the Fort Seward historic site in Jamestown, North Dakota, and the wagons travel up to 85 miles over the next six days.

The first year we went, we were surprised to find 16 states and three countries represented. Some folks came all the way from England to participate. We rode in canvas-topped, flare box wagons with wooden wheels, just like those used by the pioneers. Some folks rode horseback or walked. In fact, one woman comes every year to walk the whole thing.

The staff made all participants feel welcome. When we got there, we had orientation and were then assigned to a wagon with the folks who became our family for the week. Each wagon holds about a dozen people.

We were expected to dress the part, too, which made

Clockwise from top left: The horses graze; Katie helps teamster Dean make fry bread for supper; Anna and Katie are ready to hit the trail.

it fun. The women wore dresses and skirts, and the men wore suspenders, button-up shirts, and anything else the pioneers might have worn.

Thanks to the morning fire builders, a typical day on the trail started with a steaming cup of coffee or hot cocoa. The teamsters (expert drivers) had already been up, swapping stories with each other. Breakfast was usually at 7:30 a.m.; then we packed and loaded our bags and tents into the luggage trailer.

The teams harnessed up and the train headed out around 8:30, stopping once for a bathroom break before the noon meal. (The wagon train's rolling bathroom is called "the Biffy.")

After dinner (that's how we refer to lunch out on the wagon train), we listened to a history talk or watched a demonstration before hitting the trail again.

Around 4 in the afternoon, the wagons circled and made camp for the night. The kids played games and made crafts while supper was being made. After eating, we all sat around the campfire, singing songs, watching skits, or sharing stories until bedtime.

Some evenings featured special events. Barter Night was a favorite—riders traded items with each other just as the pioneers might have done. During the Prairie Olympics we played games like tug-of-war, competed in gunnysack races and, if we had stopped near a river, went swimming.

All this fun came with a lot of hard and rewarding work. Each person is assigned a daily chore or skill to learn, as this is a working wagon train. I learned a lot

of life lessons on this journey. The more I put into it, the more I got out of it. One day I helped with the cooking, while another day I put up the picket line for the horses and also helped to load baggage. It was fun to try a new chore every day. Until it was my turn to cook, I didn't realize just how many hands were needed or how long it took to peel potatoes for 150 people.

Although the organizers try to make everything as authentic as possible, there are some important modern conveniences. For example, a first-aid vehicle follows the train in case of any emergencies.

The only downside of the trip is the unpredictable weather! The wind and sun are intense on the Dakota prairie, and strong summer storms are also a threat, so you need good rain gear. Every year the wind puts our tents to the test!

My favorite part of the journey is all the like-minded people you meet along the way. We become like family over the course of our time together.

At the end of that first journey, I was sad that it was over, and was already planning next year's trip. I made many new friends from all over the country, traveled about 85 miles on horseback, and learned some new skills, such as how to cook over an open fire and harness a horse. When it's done, it's hard to go back to life as usual with all the modern conveniences.

It was an experience I loved, and I encourage everyone of all ages to try the Fort Seward Wagon Train. Hope to see you on the trail! ☀

Sunshine and Love

A wildflower photo brought her daughter back to her.

BY MARIE SUMNICHT *Green Bay, Wisconsin*

While the photo below speaks volumes on its own, it has a special story to go along with it. During a week while hiking with friends in Colorado, I photographed many wildflowers. But on the day I took this specific picture, God spoke to me through the image.

It was Aug. 13, 2015, the day my daughter Julia would have turned 27. She passed away 5½ years earlier. She had lived a life full of laughter, love, dance, music and more. Losing her tore my heart apart.

When I bent down to take a shot of the fireweed, I couldn't see very well through the lens. But I did make sure the flower was centered in the bright sun. Later, I looked at the image and saw this bright purple ray coming down from the sky, illuminating the flower's petals and casting the plant in a lovely glow.

My heart and mind knew immediately that God had given me a gift on Julia's birthday.

All who knew her knew that she truly epitomized the mantra Live, Love, Laugh. For that is what she did in her short 21 years.

The light reminded me of how she filled every room she entered with her very own rays of sunshine. It also reminded me that Julia is in a heavenly place full of love and beauty. ☀

Marie captured this moment while on a hike in Colorado.

Bailey Dollar bonded with her Brown Swiss steer named Goober.

Letting Go

A determined 4-H'er developed a special bond with her dairy steer.

BY BAILEY DOLLAR *Portland, Indiana*

During the past 10 years I spent as a student in 4-H, I got to work with amazing animals and supporters. But in my eighth year of showing livestock, I had a steer that topped all the others—one I'll never forget.

Ever since my earliest days of showing, I'd wanted a Brown Swiss steer. I always considered them to be the most beautiful cattle and, in my experience, they are absolute sweethearts. Well, a couple of years ago, my dad found an ad in the newspaper from someone who was selling a Brown Swiss bull. I figured if they had a bull then they had to have calves.

I called and made a reservation to pick out a calf, and eventually my dad and I made the trip. For Dad, the journey began on a frustrating note. I had told him the calf was about an hour and a half away, and the drive ended up being closer to three hours. But I'm pretty positive my happiness was enough to ease his sense of aggravation.

We finally got to the location and I was directed into a pen of three bull calves. Two of the calves lay on the ground and didn't acknowledge me, but the third was quickly by my side, covering my jeans in slobber. With a smile on my face, I looked at my dad, and without a word,

Of her many positive 4-H experiences, Bailey's time showing Goober was a highlight.

he walked over to the trailer and grabbed the halter for me.

My new calf and I walked back to the trailer not knowing how the next two years would go, but I was beyond excited for the journey.

We got the calf home, and not two hours later he had earned his name: Goober. Besides all that slobbering, he would get excited when he heard us come into the barn, and he threw a fit if we didn't show him attention.

He liked thinking that he could jump over fences and be rebellious. When I was nearby but not paying him any mind, Goober would dump his water bucket and kick the wall. He disliked halters and got grumpy when he was tied up or being taken for a walk.

But Goober was the biggest softie with my siblings and me—we could handle him without any problems at all. He was everything I had ever wanted in a steer, and we became best friends.

County fair time rolled around, and with it came some unusual challenges. For example, Goober refused to drink city water, so we had to go home and bring him water from the farm every day. To say he was spoiled is an understatement.

That year Goober took third place in the heavyweight dairy feeder steer category. We also entered the showmanship class and made it to the final cut for my age group. It was a good year for us.

The next year, fair prep began as usual. Goober learned that he could put his head under Dad's behind and lift him up when he was feeding the hogs, which pushed my dad's buttons but also put a smile on his face.

Bailey loved Goober and his consistent slobbering.

Goober had grown, and my mom's fears about me handling a big steer came back like always. He tried to eat my sister's and my hair all the time and would attempt to lick us to death. But no matter how big he got, he was still a baby.

Our last event at the fair came way too soon, and my heart felt like it would break. The idea of having to let Goober go was the only thing on my mind. Still, I hoped it would be another good year for us—but an accident at check-in nearly ruined our chances. While helping a friend check in her calf, it kicked me in the hand, and I ended up in a splint with a fractured knuckle. The doctors told me not to show Goober. They said the knuckle could end up breaking if I worked it too much.

My mom now had even more to worry about, and Dad was uneasy, too, since the injured hand was the one I needed to hold Goober's head while showing him. It would be a big challenge, but it was one I insisted on taking. I knew the only person who could show my beloved steer for the last time was me.

My dad walked Goober to the holding ring and held him until it was time to go into the show ring. It was our moment to shine.

We placed third in the finished dairy steer class and walked back into showmanship together, and with that, the part I thought was going to be the hardest was over. But then it was time to say goodbye.

Letting my friend go wasn't easy. I went with Dad to take Goober to the sale barn, and I walked him up to where he needed to go. I took his halter off, got into the truck with my dad and didn't say a word.

I will never forget Goober. People often say dogs and other small pets take a piece of your heart, but it was a big dairy steer who took mine. ☀

Sowing Seeds

This future farmer works hard.

BY SARAH EUNICE *Waynesville, Georgia*

Ethan loves working, planting and harvesting (top) and selling his crop at the Produce Shack (below).

Just off the beaten path in South Georgia's Brantley County, you'll find the Produce Shack at the Home Grown Barn. Here, our family sells a variety of seasonal produce, cane syrup, farm-fresh eggs, handcrafted signs and other knickknacks.

We think it's a local treasure, but the real gem at this place is my son, Ethan.

Though he's just 9 years old, Ethan manages the shack, which is open every other Saturday through the growing season. It's his job to water, pick the veggies, and feed the chickens, cows and goats. When we aren't open, the fruits and veggies are out on a table with a mailbox for payment (it's all on the honor system). Ethan collects and counts the money.

This hands-on experience is a good lesson for him. He's learning what it takes to run a business—hard work, dedication and math—and he is having fun doing it!

Ethan, who's been farming since age 3, loves sharing his knowledge. While in first grade, he wrote and illustrated a book, *The Growing Garden*, which is available at the Produce Shack. And he starred in a cane syrup tutorial now on YouTube.

For all his hard work, he was honored as the Brantley County Chamber of Commerce's 2018 Farmer of the Year.

His eyes lit up when he got the news. "I'm gonna have to wear a tuxedo for this," Ethan said.

When he isn't farming, Ethan enjoys attending church, playing with friends, singing, swimming, fishing, and playing baseball, football and basketball.

This farm is definitely a team effort, developed by Ethan's dad, Rowdy, and me; his brothers, Justin and Gabe; and his Grandpa Mike (with help from friends and neighbors). We are surely blessed. At the Home Grown Barn, it's more than just planting something. It's about sowing seeds for the future. ☀

Morgan and her horse, Wolfe (right, with Maddy, Jacob, Montana and Madison), won Reserve Grand Champion.

Best of Show

Happy days spent at the county fair come alive through their kids and grandchildren.

BY SUSAN TERRY *Battle Creek, Michigan*

When I was a young girl, the merry tunes of lively carnival rides and the aroma of cotton candy and caramel corn always lured me to the Calhoun County Fair in Marshall, Michigan, the state's oldest fair.

At that time, my future husband, Lloyd, was very busy showing both his dairy cows and his woodworking and gardening skills over at the Barry County Fair in Hastings, Michigan.

Once we married and our kids, Scott and Lisa, came along, we went back to the Marshall fair. Now it was the kids showing their rabbits, woodwork and baked goods. Scott won best of show for his woodwork, and Lisa won best of class for her baked goods.

A few decades later found us at the Kalamazoo County Youth Fair, where three of our grandchildren, Morgan, Jacob and Maddy, showed their horses. They also vied for ribbons in woodworking and baking, but their first love was competing in the horse arena.

They spent the early mornings feeding, grooming, mucking out stalls, cleaning tack and checking to make sure their show clothes were accounted for and clean. The events started early to give the kids—and

horses—a jump on the summer heat. (Yes, it does get hot in Michigan!)

The kids competed in English and Western, including the speed events such as barrel racing. Plus, Morgan competed in dressage and won Reserve Grand Champion at the State 4-H Show at Michigan State University. Part of the fun was that Morgan's horse was a granddaughter of Seattle Slew, the 1977 Triple Crown champ.

All the hard work, joy, sights and sounds have given us happy memories over the years. The original intent of county fairs still remains: Bringing people of all ages and diverse backgrounds together as a community to celebrate the good in our country. ☀

Maddy is super excited about winning a prize at the fair. Jacob cuts pieces for his first-year woodworking project, for which he later won a blue ribbon.

Mixing It Up with Miss Kitty

*From tennis pro to dairy farmer, she created
a place where women thrive in agriculture.*

BY BECKY SERNETT

Kitty Hockman-Nicholas took over her family's 50-acre dairy farm in Winchester, Virginia, in 1977. It was just after her brother, Robbie, died in a farm accident. She had never milked a cow before and says she knew nothing about farming at the time. Kitty was raised to be a southern lady—only boys and men went into the barn.

"But farming was always in my heart," she says.

At that time, Miss Kitty, as they call her at Hedgebrook Farm, was a professional tennis player with two young daughters, and she was going through a divorce. To be a woman and a farmer in the late 1970s was fairly unusual. At first Miss Kitty hired help for the dairy, but eventually she learned how to milk the cows herself. She replaced her father's Holsteins with Jerseys, which she jokes are "the only breed" of cow. And for the past 20 years, she's been the only one she trusts to milk the herd, which

Clockwise from left: After taking over the farm, Kitty Hockman-Nicholas brought Jerseys into the fold; Kitty and her granddaughter, Meghan Triplett, place fresh raw milk in the cooler; guests tour the farm.

consists of about 25 cows at any one time.

The family farm began as an apple orchard in 1906 and became a dairy in the 1940s. It's now a diverse and flourishing woman-owned and -operated business that produces raw milk, sells meat, provides educational programs and offers farm-stay accommodations at the Herds Inn, a two-bedroom log cabin with breathtaking views of the surrounding mountains.

Guests can pet the calves, visit the dairy, talk with Miss Kitty and delight in watching the peacocks, llamas, pigs, ducks and chickens go about their days. Kitty has also added a tiny house log cabin, the Birds Nest, sized for one or two guests or overflow from a larger group at the inn.

The dairy is the heart of the farm, though, Kitty says. And a cow boarding program, in which customers purchase part of a Jersey cow, allows Hedgebrook to produce and share raw milk. (In Virginia, it's illegal to sell raw milk.) Shares of the grass-fed, hormone- and pesticide-free milk can be picked up at the farm or delivered around the region.

Guests at Hedgebrook can stay at the Herds Inn (top); Miss Kitty; her mother, Kitty; Shannon and Meghan represented four generations of this farm family (left).

This raw milk is also used to produce cheese in the On the Farm classes offered in league with two local nonprofits, Sustainability Matters and the Lord Fairfax Soil and Water Conservation District. Engaging in such partnerships has helped diversify the farm business while honoring Kitty's passion for animal welfare, conservation and the production of high-quality food. Other partnerships at Hedgebrook Farm include a bee pollination project, a hydroponic farming system and a community garden.

Kitty's advice to her fellow farmers: "You have to be willing to change your mind away from the traditional way of farming.

"The future of farming will be corporate farms unless you, as a small farmer, are able to find more than one lucrative niche market, stay focused and build on markets with what you have."

Hedgebrook is still a family business, and Kitty gets help from her daughters, Shannon Triplett and Jackie Hott; her granddaughter, Meghan Triplett; and her grandsons, Nickolas and Griffin Hott. Kitty's mother (also named Kitty) lived on the farm until she passed away four years ago at age 98, and Kitty says she misses her every day.

Now, at age 77, Kitty sees the farm's future in its hospitality business, which her daughter Shannon helps manage.

Kitty's advice to other women who want to farm? It's simple: "Go for it." ☀

Dad the Tomato Farmer

*Crops, tractors and soil were in his father's heart,
and that love of the land was passed on.*

BY WILLIAM BRENT HECKLER *Atlanta, Georgia*

Years before I was born, my family operated a 150-acre tomato and vegetable farm in Montgomery, Pennsylvania. My grandfather, William, and father, Bill, grew tomatoes that were used by the Campbell Soup Co.

They would hitch up a team of horses twice a week and pull a wagon of fresh produce 20 miles into Philadelphia, leaving at 3 a.m. and returning well after supper. The families along their route also were thankful for the opportunity to get farm-grown vegetables.

Dad had four sisters but he carried the farming load, plowing 100 acres with horses. He wanted a tractor more than anything, and Grandfather finally relented. But the problem was, even though Dad got that shiny new tractor, my grandfather wouldn't buy gas for it. After all, hay for the horses to eat didn't cost anything.

It was World War II and rubber was in short supply. The tractor's steel wheels made it impractical to use during the rainy season. It took a year or two to get rubber tires and finally "modernize" the farm.

Dad left school in the eighth grade to tend the farm. But my mom, Ruth Miller, who grew up just around the corner on Stump Road, had gone to college like her sister and brother.

They were from very different backgrounds but Mom loved Dad, so off to the farm she went—well, for at least a little while.

One summer a blight affected the entire tomato crop. The crop could be dusted at great expense, wiping out any profit for the year, or with luck a heavy rain would wash away the blight.

My parents waited. No rain came for a week and none was in sight. So they made the call and dusted the fields.

Later that night, it rained cats and dogs. Mom had a near-death experience as a result, as my dad jokingly described it, and that was the end of her time as a farm wife. Dad began working in a hosiery mill and Mom went to a dairy.

Eventually I came along. My dad showed me how to build things, ride a horse, drive a tractor, hunt, fish and appreciate nature. I will always be a country boy at heart.

Our original farmhouse still stands, a reminder of our family's stewardship of the land. It brings memories of a simpler time. ☀

MY COUNTRY MEMORY

William Brent, at age 6, was excited to learn about Dad's farming days.

Patriotic Pops

PREP: 15 min. + freezing • **MAKES:** 1 dozen

1¾ cups vanilla yogurt, divided
2 Tbsp. honey, divided
1¼ cups sliced fresh strawberries, divided
1¼ cups fresh or frozen blueberries, thawed, divided
12 freezer pop molds or 12 paper cups (3 oz. each) and wooden pop sticks

1. Place 2 Tbsp. yogurt, 1 Tbsp. honey and 1 cup strawberries in a blender; cover and process until blended. Remove to a small bowl. Chop the remaining strawberries; stir into strawberry mixture.
2. In blender, process 2 Tbsp. yogurt, remaining honey and 1 cup blueberries until blended; remove to another bowl. Stir in remaining blueberries.
3. In each freezer pop mold, layer 1 Tbsp. strawberry mixture, 2 Tbsp. yogurt and 1 Tbsp. blueberry mixture. Top with holders. (If using paper cups, top with foil and insert sticks through the foil.) Freeze until firm.

1 pop: 55 cal., 1g fat (0 sat. fat), 2mg chol., 24mg sod., 11g carb. (10g sugars, 1g fiber), 2g pro.
Diabetic exchanges: 1 starch.

Bacon-Blue Cheese Stuffed Burgers

PREP: 30 min. • **GRILL:** 10 min. • **MAKES:** 4 servings

- 1½ lbs. lean ground beef (90% lean)
- 3 oz. cream cheese, softened
- ⅓ cup crumbled blue cheese
- ⅓ cup bacon bits
- ½ tsp. salt
- ½ tsp. garlic powder
- ¼ tsp. pepper
- 1 lb. sliced fresh mushrooms
- 1 Tbsp. olive oil
- 1 Tbsp. water
- 1 Tbsp. Dijon mustard
- 4 whole wheat hamburger buns, split
- ¼ cup mayonnaise
- 4 romaine leaves
- 1 medium tomato, sliced

1. Shape beef into 8 thin patties. Combine the cream cheese, blue cheese and bacon bits; spoon onto the center of 4 patties. Top with remaining patties and press edges firmly to seal. Combine the salt, garlic powder and pepper; sprinkle over patties.

2. Grill burgers, covered, over medium heat or broil 4 in. from the heat on each side until a thermometer reads 160° and juices run clear, 5-7 minutes.

3. Meanwhile, in a large skillet, saute mushrooms in oil until tender. Stir in water and mustard.

4. Serve burgers on buns with mayonnaise, romaine, tomato and mushroom mixture.

1 burger: 701 cal., 43g fat (15g sat. fat), 149mg chol., 1280mg sod., 31g carb. (7g sugars, 5g fiber), 48g pro.

Luscious Blueberry Jam

PREP: 20 min. • **COOK:** 20 min. + standing • **MAKES:** 8 cups

- 8 cups fresh blueberries
- 2 Tbsp. lemon juice
- 1 pkg. (1¾ oz.) powdered fruit pectin
- 7 cups sugar

1. Mash blueberries; transfer to a Dutch oven. Add lemon juice; stir in pectin. Bring to a full rolling boil over high heat, stirring constantly.

2. Stir in the sugar; return to a full rolling boil. Boil for 1 minute, stirring constantly. Remove from the heat; skim off foam. Ladle into jars or freezer containers and cool to room temperature, about 1 hour.

3. Cover and let stand overnight or until set, but not longer than 24 hours. Refrigerate for up to 3 weeks or freeze for up to 12 months.

2 Tbsp.: 95 cal., 0 fat (0 sat. fat), 0 chol., 0 sod., 25g carb. (24g sugars, 0 fiber), 0 pro.

Potluck Antipasto Pasta Salad

TAKES: 30 min. • **MAKES:** 18 servings

- 1 pkg. (16 oz.) penne pasta
- 1 can (15 oz.) garbanzo beans or chickpeas, rinsed and drained
- 1 medium sweet red or green pepper, julienned
- 2 plum tomatoes, halved lengthwise and sliced
- 1 bunch green onions, sliced
- 4 oz. Monterey Jack cheese, julienned
- 4 oz. part-skim mozzarella cheese, julienned
- 4 oz. brick or provolone cheese, julienned
- 4 oz. thinly sliced hard salami, julienned
- 3 oz. thinly sliced pepperoni
- 1 can (2¼ oz.) sliced ripe olives, drained
- 1 to 2 Tbsp. minced chives

BASIL VINAIGRETTE
- ⅔ cup canola oil
- ⅓ cup red wine vinegar
- 3 Tbsp. minced fresh basil or 1 Tbsp. dried basil
- 1 garlic clove, minced
- ¼ tsp. salt

1. Cook pasta according to package directions; rinse with cold water and drain. In a bowl, combine pasta, beans, vegetables, cheeses, meats, olives and chives.
2. In a small bowl, whisk the vinaigrette ingredients. Pour over salad; toss to coat. Cover and refrigerate. Toss before serving.

1 cup: 248 cal., 18g fat (5g sat. fat), 24mg chol., 431mg sod., 13g carb. (2g sugars, 2g fiber), 9g pro.

Cake & Berry Campfire Cobbler

PREP: 10 min. • **GRILL:** 30 min. • **MAKES:** 12 servings

- 2 cans (21 oz. each) raspberry pie filling
- 1 pkg. yellow cake mix (regular size)
- 1¼ cups water
- ½ cup canola oil
  Vanilla ice cream, optional

1. Prepare grill or campfire for low heat, using 16-20 charcoal briquettes or large wood chips.
2. Line an ovenproof Dutch oven with heavy-duty aluminum foil; add pie filling. In a large bowl, combine the cake mix, water and oil. Spread over pie filling.
3. Cover Dutch oven. When briquettes or wood chips are covered with white ash, place Dutch oven directly on top of 8-10 of them. Using long-handled tongs, place remaining briquettes on pan cover.
4. Cook until filling is bubbly and a toothpick inserted in the topping comes out clean, 30-40 minutes. To check for doneness, use the tongs to carefully lift the cover. Serve with ice cream if desired.

1 serving: 342 cal., 12g fat (2g sat. fat), 0 chol., 322mg sod., 57g carb. (34g sugars, 2g fiber), 1g pro.

Watermelon Feta Flag Salad

TAKES: 25 min. • **MAKES:** 12 servings

- ¼ cup red wine vinegar
- 1 Tbsp. Dijon mustard
- 1 Tbsp. grated lemon zest
- 1 tsp. sugar
- ¼ tsp. salt
- ¼ tsp. pepper
- ⅓ cup olive oil
- ¼ cup finely chopped red onion

SALAD
- 6 cups fresh arugula (about 5 oz.)
- 1½ cups fresh blueberries
- 5 cups cubed seedless watermelon
- 1 pkg. (8 oz.) feta cheese, cut into ½-in. cubes

1. For the vinaigrette, in a small bowl, whisk the first 6 ingredients; gradually whisk in oil until blended. Stir in onion.
2. In a large bowl, lightly toss arugula with ¼ cup vinaigrette. Arrange evenly in a large rectangular serving dish.
3. For the stars, place the blueberries over arugula at the top left corner. For the stripes, arrange watermelon and cheese in alternating rows. Drizzle with remaining vinaigrette. Serve immediately.

¾ **cup salad:** 140 cal., 10g fat (4g sat. fat), 17mg chol., 256mg sod., 10g carb. (7g sugars, 1g fiber), 4g pro.

Salmon with Honey Pecan Sauce

TAKES: 30 min. · **MAKES:** 4 servings

- 4 **salmon fillets (4 oz. each)**
- ½ **tsp. seasoned salt**
- ¼ **tsp. pepper**
- ¼ **cup finely chopped pecans, toasted**
- ¼ **cup honey**
- 3 **Tbsp. reduced-fat butter**

1. Sprinkle salmon with seasoned salt and pepper. Place fish on oiled grill rack, skin side down. Grill, covered, over medium-high heat or broil 4 in. from heat until fish just begins to flake easily with a fork, 6-8 minutes.

2. Meanwhile, in a small saucepan, cook the pecans, honey and butter over medium heat until bubbly, about 5-7 minutes. Serve with salmon.

NOTE This recipe was tested with Land O'Lakes light stick butter.

1 fillet with 2 Tbsp. sauce: 330 cal., 20g fat (5g sat. fat), 68mg chol., 319mg sod., 19g carb. (18g sugars, 1g fiber), 20g pro.
Diabetic exchanges: 3 lean meat, 2½ fat, 1 starch.

Peanut Butter Icebox Dessert

PREP: 20 min. + chilling · **MAKES:** 15 servings

- 1 pkg. (8 oz.) peanut butter sandwich cookies, crushed, divided
- ¼ cup sugar
- ¼ cup butter, melted
- 1 pkg. (8 oz.) cream cheese, softened
- 1⅓ cups confectioners' sugar
- 1 carton (8 oz.) frozen whipped topping, thawed, divided
- 2½ cups cold 2% milk
- 2 pkg. (3.9 oz. each) instant chocolate pudding mix

1. In a large bowl, combine 1¾ cups crushed cookies, sugar and butter; press into an ungreased 13x9-in. baking dish. Bake at 350° 6-8 minutes or until golden brown; cool on a wire rack.
2. In a large bowl, beat the cream cheese and confectioners' sugar until smooth; fold in 1½ cups whipped topping. Spread over cooled crust.
3. In another large bowl, beat milk and pudding mix on low speed until thickened, about 2 minutes. Spread over cream cheese layer. Top with remaining whipped topping; sprinkle with ¼ cup crushed cookie pieces. Cover and refrigerate for at least 1 hour before serving.

1 piece: 323 cal., 15g fat (9g sat. fat), 27mg chol., 217mg sod., 43g carb. (31g sugars, 1g fiber), 4g pro.

Dilly Potato & Egg Salad

PREP: 20 min. + chilling · **COOK:** 20 min. + cooling
MAKES: 12 servings

- 4 lbs. medium red potatoes (about 14), peeled and halved
- 5 hard-boiled large eggs
- 1 cup chopped dill pickles
- 1 small onion, chopped
- 1½ cups mayonnaise
- 1 tsp. celery seed
- ½ tsp. salt
- ¼ tsp. pepper
  Paprika

1. Place potatoes in a large saucepan; add water to cover. Bring to a boil. Reduce heat; cook, uncovered, until tender, 15-20 minutes. Drain; cool completely.
2. Cut potatoes into ¾-in. cubes; place in a large bowl. Chop 4 eggs; slice remaining egg. Add chopped eggs, pickles and onion to potatoes. Mix mayonnaise, celery seed, salt and pepper; stir gently into potato mixture. Top with sliced egg and sprinkle with paprika. Refrigerate, covered, at least 2 hours before serving.

¾ cup: 326 cal., 22g fat (4g sat. fat), 80mg chol., 413mg sod., 25g carb. (2g sugars, 3g fiber), 6g pro.

HANDCRAFTED WITH LOVE

Place Mats

Perfect the picnic table with cute and functional table settings.

WHAT YOU'LL NEED
- ½ yd. denim fabric
- Heavy-duty thread
- Back pocket from old jeans
- Sewing machine
- Iron

DIRECTIONS
1. Cut denim to preferred place mat size, about 12x18 in. Using heavy-duty thread, sew a ½-in. border around denim.
2. Iron mat and trim any loose strings.
3. Sew pocket on three sides to lower-right side of mat, keeping top open. Sew along existing stitching on pocket. Tuck silverware and a napkin in pocket.

Vacation in a Jar

Preserve the fun of a family trip
in a Mason jar.

WHAT YOU'LL NEED

- Quart-sized Mason jar with vintage lid
- Soil or sand collected from vacation
- Printed photo
- Small travel souvenirs
- Miniatures, optional
- Card stock
- Twine or ribbon
- Scissors
- Paint pen

DIRECTIONS

1. Fill the bottom of a Mason jar with some soil or sand. Be sure to practice Leave No Trace principles while collecting. Visit *lnt.org* for more information.
2. Arrange photo in jar as a backdrop.
3. Embellish with travel souvenirs and miniatures, if desired, to complete scene.
4. Cut a tag out of card stock. Write vacation location and date on tag with paint pen. Arrange in jar, or adhere to outside. Top jar with lid and decorative twine or ribbon.

Mason Jar Luminaries

These festive night lights are
as much fun as the fireworks.

WHAT YOU'LL NEED

- 3 jar lids with wire hangers
- Spray paint, optional
- 3 quart-sized Mason jars
- Star stickers or a star template and adhesive sheet
- Red, white and blue acrylic craft paint
- Decoupage glue
- 3 tea lights or three strings of battery-operated mini lights
- Small paintbrush

DIRECTIONS

1. Spray-paint lids, if desired. Dry thoroughly.
2. Using template, if needed, cut out star stickers from adhesive sheet. Cover the jars in a decorative pattern with stickers.
3. Paint one jar red, one white and one blue with the acrylic paint. Dry thoroughly. Repeat with a second coat of paint.
4. Carefully remove stickers. Touch up paint as needed and dry thoroughly.
5. Paint a coat of the decoupage glue over each jar and dry thoroughly.
6. Insert lights into jars. Top with lids.

Autumn

The Black River gently cascades in
Wisconsin's Pattison State Park.
PHOTO BY TERRY DONNELLY

THE GOOD LIFE

Our Gathering Place

*The doors are always open for life lessons
or a cup of coffee at her grandparents' farm.*

BY DEBBIE BETTS *Dansville, New York*

Many people don't realize all the behind-the-scenes effort it takes to grow what we eat on a daily basis. A lot of hours and sweat go into being a farmer.

But no matter how busy my grandma and grandpa were running their farm, they always made time for family. Their example taught me so much. Like them, I would do anything for my family and I have a lot of pride in my farming heritage.

Although my grandparents are both gone, my mom and her sister still live on their land. They collect more than a dozen fresh eggs daily from the chickens they raise. They also keep geese and plant a huge garden every year.

I live an hour away on my own little farm, but I visit Mom's place just about every weekend. My kids go to their grandma's house all the time, too. I hope they learn the same life lessons that I did from my time as a child on the farm.

The legacy first began when my grandpa Lewis Frey bought his 50-plus-acre farm with two barns, several outbuildings and a huge house in Macedon, New York, in 1938. The following November he brought his bride, Dorothy, to join him and make a homestead.

At first Grandpa made his living by raising replacement heifers for local dairy farmers and growing cash crops such as carrots. When his three children (my mom and her brother and sister) came along in the 1940s, he sought some additional employment in the nearby city of Rochester. When I was growing up he was retired but still working on the farm.

Through the years Grandpa and Grandma raised many kinds of animals: cows, horses, turkeys, chickens, ducks, geese, pigs and an occasional goat or pony. They also planted a garden that provided an abundant harvest for Grandma to can or freeze for the winter.

When Grandma and Grandpa first moved to the farm, Grandma invited her younger brothers to stay during the summer. My mom's cousins also came and stayed there for weeks on end.

Grandpa Lewis Frey on his farm in 1940.

Continuing the tradition, my generation of cousins spent our weekends and summers on the farm. My dad passed away when I was about 4 years old, and my aunt was also a single mother with young children. My mom and her sister loved farm life and knew it was a great place for us, too.

Along the way we were taught wonderful life lessons such as the value of hard work, humility, responsibility, independence and compassion for animals.

My grandparents always needed help with weeding the garden or getting in hay. One of my most cherished memories is when my cousins and I would drive the old two-cylinder John Deere tractor and the adults would go

along and pick up the bales off the ground to stack them on the wagon.

Grandma and Grandpa made everyone feel welcome as they hosted extended family picnics, and baby and bridal showers. Family and friends would stop by year-round just to visit, either under the lean-to or inside the house, but always for a cup of coffee. Sometimes they would stay long enough to play cards.

My cousins and I celebrated our birthdays and the holidays at the farm as kids, and we still do. All of us cousins gather there for picnics in the summer. And family and friends continue to stop by just to visit. The coffee's always on! ☀

Clockwise from top: The Frey farm; Peter relaxes by the creek; Peter plants a garden with cousin Mary; Debbie's children, Peter, Abbey and Andrew, with their cousin Trevor (holding loppers) in the patch.

My Life with Chickens

*She went from loathing chickens
to caring for them full time.*

BY AMARA L. BIEDLER *Westville, Oklahoma*

The Biedler family (far left) work together on their Oklahoma farm to care for their 10,000 hens. Amara's special relationship with feathered friends (left and below) was apparent from an early age.

Every little girl dreams of the day when she will grow up, meet her fabled farmer on his trusty, rusty tractor and ride off into the sunset to the land of chickens and eggs. Wait—that's not how it goes?

Right, it wasn't like that for me either. But it's the happily ever after I am living. And I'm glad it is—but it wasn't always so.

As a preschooler, I spent a lot of time in my California backyard with a bucket, grubbing snails to give to our neighbor's white duck, Webster. Webster adored snails and gobbled them gratefully, and the neighbors let my cousin and me eat one of their duck eggs. It was my very first taste of fresh eggs.

Then we moved, which began a series of relocations throughout my childhood, each one bringing a new bird experience: There was Emma, a sweet turkey from a nearby farm. An adopted pet rooster named Clementine who was a bully-turned-friend after I overcame my fear and stood up to him. Then there was the flock of Muscovy ducks we raised, the Canada geese and blue herons that visited our pond, the ducks I played with at the docks, and all the injured birds and fallen nestlings we saved. I loved almost any creature I came across.

When I was 12, following moves to Florida and North Carolina, our family headed next to a 350-acre farm in West Virginia.

This new farm life allowed us to have our own chickens and raise our own meat birds for the freezer. My dad built a clever raised chicken run and a little chicken house with a door that opened behind the nests for easy egg-collecting. We named some of our chickens after *Gone with the Wind* characters and others according to whatever story or movie theme we thought of at the time.

We had fun entering our prized fowl in the county fair, and racked up ribbons of all sorts. At first I really enjoyed gathering the eggs, but I soon found cleaning the houseful of messy birds to be an icky task.

Eventually, my dad had to take a job that took him away from the farm, and the bulk of the chores were left to my mother, sister and me. But with all the muck, feathers and day-to-day slogging between the farm chores and birds, my joy in chickens began to wane. By the time my family moved to the suburbs after 10th grade, I decided that I was done with poultry altogether. Never again, I said.

Then I met this boy. A boy who loved the country and was as smart as they come. A boy with more than a

From left: The Biedler children—Miles, Mariel, Miriam and Matthias—have been a part of their parents' farm dreams since the beginning; husband Mark prepares pallets of eggs for another pickup.

pocketful of innovative dreams of his own. And he swept me off my feet and into a lifetime of adventure.

After college and six brief moves, we ended up in Illinois with a 1-year-old, a 2-week-old, and a house of dreams nestled on 1 acre with a small farm to the south, a country neighborhood to the west and north, and a cornfield stretching off to the east. It was the perfect haven to start our family life, which soon grew to four darling rascals under the age of 4. We explored, gardened, fixed up our nearly 90-year-old farmhouse, and let the munchkins climb trees and come home wild and happy with purple hands from munching freshly picked mulberries.

We eventually branched out into mini-homesteading, something I had long dreamed about. We got a milk cow, rabbits and a pony. And in all that country fun I realized that we had room for chickens. Even if I didn't like them. Even if the thought of them was still gross to me. I know I once said never again, but...this was a new era. What a neat experience it would be for the children to have chicks of their own! So I broached the subject, and my husband, Mark, agreed. We were ready to embark on our new chicken journey.

In time, we realized our 1-acre world in Illinois just wasn't big enough for all we wanted to do. So we moved out to Oklahoma and settled into a little green house on 54 acres with a gorgeous creek running beside the property. Within four days of our arrival we bought a nanny goat and her darling kid—we just couldn't help ourselves! Then one month later we bought 15 calves; a month after that we bought four piglets; six months after that we added some ducks and the chickens, and eventually included a flock of gobbling, gorgeous and rather troublesome turkeys.

Yes, we rarely do anything in half measures. It's both a blessing and a curse, believe me! But it was a new world, full of new possibilities. So after spending a few months helping out with some new friends' laying hens, an idea was planted: Maybe we could do this, too?

The opportunity to sell eggs to the same company as our friends presented itself, and we spent much of 2016 making it become a reality. We added 10,000 pastured laying hens and miles of fencing to the property, with the ultimate goal of Mark being able to farm full time rather than just part time.

I never in my wildest dreams imagined we would own two barns full of clucking, fluttering birds and walk through those buildings every day, collecting 9,500 eggs. But life changes, and sometimes with it, your priorities change, too. You see things differently and with a lot more clarity than you did as a kid. God certainly has a sense of humor!

These chickens are actually really rather interesting and amazing creatures (despite their inherently flighty ways), and we're really enjoying learning how to expand our plans from small-flock to large-flock husbandry. The chickens' silly ways amuse us often—they'll sometimes even perch on top of us as we work with the feeding and watering equipment. I think my perspective on chickens has officially come full circle.

Most importantly, these chickens have become a wonderful means to an end. Mark is now a full-time farmer, just as we dreamed. We have a contract with an egg company that purchases all our eggs and picks them up weekly. Each pallet holds 10,800 eggs, and we usually have five to six pallets ready for pickup. The company then washes, sorts and packages the eggs for stores.

Best of all, it's something we all get to do as a family: continuing to grow our farm while including our kids in this future.

With chickens. Lots and lots of chickens.

If that's not happily ever after, I don't know what is. ☀

Raising Cane the Old-Fashioned Way

A holiday morning tradition brings together family.

BY KARIE CHATHAM *Mount Olive, Mississippi*

If you ask Evans and Johnny Miller how long they've been growing sugar cane and making homemade syrup out of it, they'll tell you they reckon it's been their whole lives.

When fall descends in the Deep South and the leaves start to change colors, my Grandfather Evans and Great-Uncle Johnny know it's almost time for cane. Cane grows from fall to fall, and it never needs to be replanted after it's chopped down. Starting a new patch of sugar cane is easy, though, because you can simply lay a cane stick on the ground and nature will do its job from there.

Over the years, the brothers have included their sons in the cane tradition, and later their grandsons joined in. Every Thanksgiving morning, the brothers, sons and grandsons—along with additional family and friends—come together on the Miller family farm in Bassfield, Mississippi, to make the syrup.

The family uses stripping tools to remove the cane leaves, cut off the tops and cut the stalks down before bundling them together. Next, the sugar cane stalks are taken to a mill. Traditionally, a mule or a horse would have kept the mill going, but today they use tractors.

Johnny has a mill in his backyard that grinds the stalks. After they're ground, the juice is drained and strained before it's poured into a giant syrup pan. The syrup is cooked while someone monitors it closely, continually skimming the foam off the top.

From there, the syrup is poured into jars and divided up, some going to the family and some to be given away as gifts. The family turns 100 gallons of juice into about 20 gallons of syrup every year.

The sweet reward for all their hard work is a delicious syrup that is poured over biscuits throughout the next year, until harvesttime comes around again. ☀

Clockwise from above left: A lot of work goes into getting a finished jar of pure cane syrup; Evans Miller (middle of back row) poses with grandsons (from left) Fisher Miller, Jake Miller and John Daniel Ellis, along with his brother, Johnny (back right); generations of the Miller family harvest sugar cane.

Henry and Sofia relax with dog Daisy Rose after chores.

We're All in This Together

Oklahoma welcomed their family to a small rural homestead.

BY NINA CASON *Coweta, Oklahoma*

It seems like we had to take a long trip and travel around the whole world before we finally found our home and settled down in Wagoner County, Oklahoma. The journey started in England, where I was born, when I met and married Jeff, who was from rural Ohio.

He had moved to Manchester to help start a church in 1998. I met Jeff in the first two weeks he was there. We married about 18 months later, in 1999, and in 2003 we took off and were barely home for close to two years. We traveled through Asia, the Middle East and Europe before returning to England, which is where our daughter Sofia was born.

There we lived in a city of over 3 million people with never a moment's silence. So when the ministry asked us in 2007 to pack up and move to Oklahoma to help with their office, we headed there in pursuit of a simpler, quieter life. Soon after we arrived, Jeff had to find other employment and returned to the electrical work he had

done before moving to England.

For a while we lived in a two-room converted barn—there were still horse stalls below us. Although it was small and primitive, we'd never trade our "barn years." They helped us be grateful for how far we have come. And we expanded our family with another daughter, Evie, and a son, Henry.

Most weekends were spent looking for a permanent home. Then one day I saw that an interesting property had just become available about 20 minutes away and drove by the house. The owner was out in the yard so I stopped to talk to her, and that was it. We'd finally found the place where we belonged.

The first few weeks in our new ranch-style home were fun. Going from 700 square feet to double that, we kept losing each other!

Our favorite feature is a wood-burning stove, which we use 24 hours a day during the frigid winter months. But while we'd looked for a house to decorate and put

Clockwise from top left: A few of the farm's chickens; Jeff and Nina with their children, from left, Sofia, Evie and Henry; Sofia snuggles a kid.

food self-sufficient. Each year, the garden gets bigger. We raise goats for meat and milk, chickens for eggs and meat, bees for honey, and turkeys for the holidays. I use some of our goats' milk to make soaps and lotions, which I sell at the farmers market and on our farm's website.

Our wonderful friends have truly taken us under their wing and shown us what it means to be an Okie. They're compassionate, kind, caring and generous. It's nice to sit with them under the shade tree during the summer or gather around a barrel fire in the winter.

We have no relatives nearby in Oklahoma, but we have lovely neighbors. And our family has a strong bond and an attitude that we are in this together.

I give back to my community wherever possible. I teach cooking classes at the library, and I also have a cooking segment on a local morning TV news show, *Good Day Tulsa*, which is so much fun.

Jeff volunteers as Santa in the Christmas parade. Our kids love seeing him waving at the crowds from up in a firetruck.

Although we're just a few miles from Coweta, a Tulsa suburb with some 10,000 residents along the Arkansas River, about the only thing that interrupts the silence is the rooster crowing or goat kids calling for their mamas.

In England I had no idea that I craved the life of a goat farmer, gardener, home-schooler and homesteader. If I have learned one lesson from our cross-continents move, it is that if we stay open to new things, God will direct our path. And this country life sure is a good one. ☀

our mark on, we have barely touched the inside. Instead, we've spent a lot of time on the outside of the property.

Even before we fully unpacked, we started a small garden and ate lots of cucumbers and summer squash that first summer. And we refenced almost a half-mile around our 3-acre homestead, Farm Sweet Farm, which was a labor of love.

We are working toward our goal of being completely

Vintage Visions

*A childhood dream kept this old farmhouse
from being put out to pasture.*

BY RACHAEL LISKA

A newly constructed home with perfect floors and freshly painted drywall is a dream come true for most people. Taylor Mimnaugh has a different dream, especially when it comes to forgotten farmhouses. She hears the old stories behind the splintered wood and sees potential under the layers of peeling paint.

She's a mother of four young children, and someone may think her life would be too busy to take on a major renovation project. There's a 1920s farmhouse in Cushing, Wisconsin, that would tell you otherwise. Just take a stroll through its kitchen—once worn-out, it's now a welcoming space, built through hours of love, care and labor.

"Ever since I was a little girl, it's been a dream of mine to own an old farmhouse," Taylor says. "So when a family friend told us his parents' home was for sale, a place I remembered from childhood, it seemed a blessing. My husband, Alex, and I knew it needed work, but our young family was the one meant to breathe life back into it."

Taylor's vision for this particular kitchen was to design and create something that would keep the home's history intact while being light, airy and functional for today's family. "I wanted someone to walk in and never know that the kitchen wasn't original to the farmhouse," Taylor says. "But I still wanted to enjoy amenities like a dishwasher and a modern stove and refrigerator."

The Mimnaughs gutted the space and donated the 1980s-era solid wood cabinets to Habitat for Humanity. Starting fresh allowed for a new design, one that was more true to the farmhouse's original time period.

"I designed the cabinets and my dad, who owns a cabinet shop in Minnesota, built them," Taylor says. Taylor's dad also made butcher block countertops by hand. For hardware, they chose old-style latches and drawer pulls common in older kitchens.

Like any prepared farm girl, Taylor knows the work is never done. "Saving this old farmhouse has been a dream come true," she says. "My goal, however, is to save farmhouses all over, restoring them to their original beauty for others to enjoy." ☀

A Home for All Seasons

She loves to watch nature throughout the year, from hummingbirds to snowflakes.

BY LINDA BAUER *Libby, Montana*

When I retired in 2014, my husband, Gary, and I decided to relocate from central Montana to the northwest corner of Big Sky Country.

One day Gary and I drove along a curvy driveway back to a house we were scheduled to see. The view was spectacular. We loved this place even before we got inside, and knew the search for our dream home was over. We now live in what we think is the most beautiful area of our state.

Our property consists of mostly evergreen forest. The front yard was cleared of most of the trees to open it to the beautiful view of the expansive Cabinet Mountains. The yard is a mix of native grasses and clover, plus areas we've left natural that bloom with pink shooting stars, yellow arrowleaf balsamroot, purple lupines and other pretty wildflowers. We have left our property natural so that it stays a habitat for many birds and animals. Our visitors include wild turkeys, squirrels, rabbits and deer.

Through all seasons, our region of Montana is known for outdoor recreation in the Cabinets, from hiking and fishing to snowshoeing. There's always a reason to enjoy the great outdoors.

One of my favorite times of the year here is mid-May, when the hummingbirds show up. I can sit for hours watching the hummers feed and fight at the feeders.

I planted a garden of perennials beside our deck. The lavender, coneflowers, peonies, salvia and columbines draw both hummers and butterflies. When the chive plant flowers, it attracts many types of bees. I included some birdbaths in the garden, because natural sources of water for the wildlife tend to dry up as the summer's heat intensifies.

During summer, the view changes. The snow in the mountains moves to higher elevations or disappears, depending on the temperature. Our native grasses brown as they enter a dormant phase. A few years ago our view was of wildfires in the mountains behind our house.

My favorite view is in the fall, when the larch trees (a deciduous conifer) turn yellow before they drop their needles. The mountains glow golden in the sunshine. Rain might come, along with some clouds and fog. The Steller's jays visit for a short time.

As winter comes, we watch the snow start in the higher elevations, move into the lower elevations and finally arrive in our area. We put up bird feeders for the nuthatches, chickadees, downy woodpeckers and other hardy species that live here through the winter.

To prepare for the snowy days ahead, Gary and I get out the snowplow, snowblower, snowshoes and cross-country skis. We drink coffee and tea by our fireplace and watch the snow fall.

The seasons come and go here at our home in Libby, Montana, but no matter what weather nature gives us, we always enjoy and appreciate our year-round views! ☀

Linda's Montana home is a sanctuary where she can relax outdoors and watch the critters and birds that visit her natural gardens. In winter (above), she cross-country skis in her backyard with its gorgeous mountain views.

CAPTURE THE BEAUTY AROUND YOU

SCRAPBOOK

As days grow shorter and cooler, crisp breezes send painted leaves dancing along the back roads. I bask in the beauty that is autumn in the country.
JONI YATES *Fulton, Kentucky*

Eli and Levi, my identical twins, love playing together. I snapped this photo
of the two of them goofing around by my autumn decorations.
NIKKI PULLEY *Dickson, Tennessee*

I've seen many moose over the years while visiting Grand Teton National Park, but never like this. The big guy just walked right out into the beautiful morning light and before I knew it, he was gone.
DAVE GISH *Wilton, Connecticut*

The scenery on the way up Mount Katahdin in Maine was amazing. I was so blessed to go with my brother.
THOMAS JONES *Pennellville, New York*

This blue jay had been eluding me all summer, but I was finally in the right place one fall day.
BONNIE SCHNABL *Sullivan, Wisconsin*

The joy on my daughter Fraya's face was priceless while gathering apples at my Aunt Gina's orchard.
NATASHA ADAMS *Lake View, Iowa*

I was driving on a seldom-used gravel road near the Wyoming border, south of Spearfish, South Dakota. As I rounded a curve, I immediately knew this scene just begged to be photographed.
KERDALL REMBOLDT *Rapid City, South Dakota*

Looks like I put the hummingbird feeder a little too close to the fence for these cows!
SHEILA BABIN *Orange, Texas*

My son Carson was intently trying to figure out who this guy was at the local pumpkin patch.
MAEGAN STAUFFER *Findlay, Ohio*

We traveled to Virginia's Shenandoah National Park for vacation, and my son Titus asked me to get a picture of him "holding onto the sun."
MELISSA KORNBAU *Cook Station, Missouri*

Yellowstone was my first national park, and it's still my favorite after many visits. I saw these majestic elk in an open field near the Madison River.
BRENT YOUNG *Pleasant Grove, Utah*

Wild mustangs are part of our American heritage. Every time I photograph them, I am moved by their beauty and grace. This white stallion was eating moss as the sun came up over the Salt River in Arizona.
JERRY COWART *Chatsworth, California*

My grandpa Cleo Ford bought our family farm in upstate New York 60 years ago. He still likes to help out!
KERYSA FORD *Ooltewah, Tennessee*

I've been taking my son Walker's picture in the fall leaves ever since he was a baby!
SHYLA WOLF *Newton Falls, Ohio*

Our family's dachshund, Romy, used to be scared of pumpkins, but now she enjoys these giant objects!
MORGAN SWART *Yukon, Oklahoma*

My friend Adam lost his battle with cancer a few days before I took this photo.
Adam also loved capturing the beauty of nature with his camera.
KALLIE KANTOS *International Falls, Minnesota*

John Tanner of Proctorville, Ohio, here with his
grandson, Tanner, made and hung this barn quilt.
GERALDINE TANNER *Chillicothe, Ohio*

My grandson Kanekoa was mesmerized by the
bounty after he went apple picking!
JANICE WEATHERSBY *Lake Wales, Florida*

The stable where I ride horses is beautiful in fall, with all the changing maples.
This old Farmall tractor is still used at the barn every day!
SOMMER SHEHADEH *Royal Oak, MIchigan*

Every season is photogenic at Oak Openings Preserve Metropark
in Swanton, Ohio, but none is more colorful than fall.
MICHELLE TERRY *Kent, Ohio*

Tradition being passed to the next generation—if you look closely, you'll see a boy sitting on a man's lap.
CHRISTA STERKEN *Queen Creek, Arizona*

My husband, Phil, and I spotted this critter on our autumn trip to the Colorado Rocky Mountains.
TAMI GINGRICH *Middlefield, Ohio*

My husband, Ted, grew a 43-pound pumpkin. I just love that smile!
VIRGINIA DAGGETT *Joseph, Oregon*

The Doane cousins, ages 2 to 20, line up for a Thanksgiving portrait on my brother-in-law's farm in Virginia.
KAY DOANE *Carriere, Mississippi*

Every November, sandhill cranes migrate to the
Bosque del Apache National Wildlife Refuge.
KARIN LEPERI *Placitas, New Mexico*

Our granddaughters Krislin, Erica and Jenna show
off the enormous sweet potatoes we grew.
CORINNE AND LON BOWMAN *Bradford, Ohio*

The fall season is reflected in this broken farm outbuilding window like stained glass.
Nature never misses an opportunity to show off!
TOM GRIFFITHE *Anaheim Hills, California*

Restoration Runs in the Family

Her kids rehabbed a rare tractor to honor those fighting an all-too-common disease.

BY JULIE PETERSEN *Knoxville, Iowa*

When she was 17, our daughter, Jenny, restored a 1967 John Deere 2510 tractor for her FFA project. To honor her grandmother, aunt and anyone else who has been impacted by breast cancer, she decided to paint it pink. Her grandma had been a breast cancer survivor for 35 years.

Having restored a '67 Deere for his own FFA project, our son Joshua had more painting experience, so he helped out by giving Jenny's tractor its pink finish.

Our family originally bought the tractor from our neighbor. We did not realize how rare 2510 tractors were until we decided to restore this one. Deere only made them for three years, and only about 8,000 are gas syncro like ours. Now it's pink and rare!

After Jenny finished restoring it, she exhibited the tractor at the Iowa State Fair. And in 2014 and 2016, she took her "li'l pink tractor" to our state Capitol building during the Race for the Cure walk for breast cancer awareness.

In 2019, Jenny finished her third year at Iowa State University, majoring in agricultural and life sciences education and minoring in entrepreneurial studies. As a 4-H alumna and a member of FFA, Jenny loves showing sheep at state, national and jackpot shows. She has her own flock and raises show lambs.

My husband, James, and I are so very proud of our son and daughter for their hard work on these tractors. We are equally proud of our two older sons, Justin and Jacob, who work on our very busy Petersen Family Farms. We raise more than 1,000 sheep and 300 head of cattle and grow corn, soybeans, oats and hay. God has blessed us. ☀

Jenny Petersen first showed her tractor at the Iowa State Fair. These days she raises and exhibits sheep through her Royalty Show Lambs.

There's plenty of flour and silliness when Woodson, Mawmaw, Anna and Karie get together.

Sleepover at Mawmaw's

She's grateful for family, bedtime stories and homemade dumplings.

BY ANNA ELLIS *Collins, Mississippi*

Every Thanksgiving I thank God for all the fun memories and many laughs I share with my family. That's why we have Thanksgiving—to be thankful for life's many blessings!

The day before the holiday, my older cousin Karie and I go to church with my grandmother. When we get back to Mawmaw's house, we sit down on the living room floor and play board games.

Finally, Mawmaw tells us that we need to get to bed. Karie and I put on our pajamas and snuggle up under the covers. I beg Karie to tell me a story. When she does, I listen. She is a wonderful storyteller, and I lie there fascinated as she tells one tale after another.

As I look back, every story she has told had a wonderful moral, whether it was about sharing, listening or keeping promises. After she finishes one story, I plead for "just one more." After about three stories, we tell each other "good night" and turn out the light.

The next morning, Karie and I wake up to the smell of bacon frying. Mawmaw makes a hearty breakfast of bacon, eggs, grits and biscuits. It's a real feast! Later, we pull out the pot and begin working together to make our specialty—dumplings.

Mawmaw or Karie prepares the dough, and I knead it. Then, with Karie's help, I roll out the dough and cut it into squares. Mawmaw drops them in the pot of boiling chicken broth.

Throughout the morning, we cook pies, cakes, ham and turkey. At around 11 a.m., the rest of the family begins coming in, bringing rolls, dressing and so much more yummy food. My family spends the day talking, laughing and eating together.

Three years after this tradition began, we now have three kids spending the night with Mawmaw before Thanksgiving: Karie, my cousin Woodson and me.

I really don't know how the three of us sleep on that full-size bed. It's a miracle one of us doesn't wake with bruises from falling off! I think sometimes Karie sleeps on the couch—bless her heart. Either way, with two cousins, it's double the fun! ☀

As an old barn comes down, Angela (left) and her friend Lisa Wilson carefully move the lumber.

One Board at a Time

With an idea and a love of barns, this entrepreneur launched a business to preserve farming heritage.

BY ANGELA CROUSE *Shelbyville, Indiana*

The thought was a simple one: I would do what I loved, and then share that love with others. Boy, how that snowballed!

I live on a farm, and I've always admired old barns. Haylofts fill my mind with memories. I also have a passion for gatherings and sharing meals.

I knew the market for quality farm tables was a good one. But to sell them, I had to make them. *How hard can it be?* I wondered.

Fast-forward three years: I now run my own business, Reclaimed Barns & Beams. With the help and support of my family and a small but mighty crew, I reclaim old barns and then sell the lumber or use it to build furniture and other items for homes and businesses.

There are lots of beautiful barns in central Indiana, and so many are falling to the ground. They have stood in the fields—often for well over a century—but they no longer meet their owners' needs.

This means a tremendous amount of quality lumber is being lost. I had stumbled across an opportunity to make a difference and save pieces of our agricultural heritage before it was too late.

The timing of my venture was perfect, as I was ready to leave the corporate world. I didn't want to miss yet another family dinner because I was stuck in a meeting.

My first project was a 45-foot-tall gambrel dairy barn. The owner said I could have all of the wood. It had 90-year-old oak beams and floor joists, and it was covered in weathered pine shiplap siding.

The size of the barn was daunting, but the crew and I focused on one board at a time. We rented lifts and used any tools that made the job easier.

Clockwise from top left: Angela climbs to saw beams; barn wood warms the Animal Eye Clinic in Westfield; taking photos in an important step before Angela starts to work because barns hold so many memories.

I filled buildings on my own farm with the reclaimed lumber. Next, I took on the laborious task of removing nails from the wood. Then the wood was trimmed and sanded to prepare it for homes and businesses. Beams were kiln-dried and readied for their next purpose as a mantel or as part of a ceiling.

The business has grown more than I ever imagined. The crew and I finished taking down that first barn, plus eight others, and we have a list of barns yet to reclaim. Calls, emails and orders have come in from as far away as California and New Jersey.

The biggest lesson I've learned as an entrepreneur is that you cannot do everything on your own. You have to know your strengths and connect with others who have skills that complement yours.

I also ask a lot of questions and am honest about how much I don't know. I've learned to speak "mill talk" and identify wood, work with it and create beautiful pieces.

Within a short time I opened both a woodshop and a lumberyard. From there I added a second location and a brick-and-mortar store with a showroom for customers.

My favorite thing about my job is knowing that I can take lumber from these old barns and pass it along to future generations. I create mantels, farm tables, paneling, shelving and more, and I sell raw lumber for others' projects.

As I walk through an old milking barn with someone who's decided to let it go, I think, *I am so grateful to do work that I love.* ☀

Stitching the Family Archive

Her Thanksgiving tablecloth spells out 17 years of holiday gatherings.

BY DEB WOODS MILLS *Clinton, Missouri*

When my husband, David, and I married, we blended five children into one big family. We have since welcomed into the fold 11 grandchildren, ages 1 to 27, plus one great-grandchild.

I'd heard of events involving signatures on tablecloths, and it sounded like a good idea. So 17 years ago I put an off-white tablecloth on the Thanksgiving table. Our kids thought I was crazy when I first asked them to sign it.

Since then, all Thanksgiving guests have signed the tablecloth with a special fabric marker that disappears in the wash. I put the cloth away until January, and then during the winter months I embroider it, using a different color each year.

Early on, if the kids broke up with their sweethearts, they'd ask if I would remove the stitching of those names. I told them no, they had to be selective about who they invited to dinner. We joke about strategically placing the gravy boat over a few names, but the bottom line is that everyone on our tablecloth is important to us, even if they're no longer part of our tribe. There are probably close to 350 names now.

When the grands arrive for Thanksgiving, I often find them gathered around the table trying to find their names from earlier years. To help keep everything straight, I embroidered a color key around the edge of the cloth.

As time passes, the value of the tablecloth increases. It is so special to have the signatures of those who have been dear to us but are no longer here—including my mom, David's father and our eldest daughter, Mary, whom we lost in 2014. When I pull the cloth out each year and see her name, it feels like she's still with us.

Along with the names there are milestones, too: a graduation cap, the footprint of a newborn grandchild, handprints. A few years ago when I sat down to embroider, I found a message from our then-8-year-old grandson: "I love Grammy and Papa." Last year, our pregnant daughter-in-law drew a baby next to her name.

During a conversation, our eldest granddaughters recently said they'd learn to embroider so they could eventually start tablecloth traditions of their own. And that's really what it's all about: making treasures for the next generation and memories to last. ☀

Our Perfect Day

A family outing to the local farm harvests acres of happy memories.

BY SUZANNE BALL *Manhattan, Illinois*

Two fun traditions exemplify fall in rural Illinois: corn mazes and pumpkin patches. Every weekend families head to a local farm to enjoy the simple pleasures of being outdoors before winter sets in. For our family, there's no better way to spend an afternoon than at Rader Family Farms in Normal, Illinois. We put on old sweaters and shoes that don't mind a little mud—it can get sloppy in those fields!

The farm has been owned and operated by the same hardworking family for generations. The Raders started with dairy cows, then became grain farmers. Ten years ago, they added corn mazes and pumpkin patches. Today they grow 12 acres for a corn maze, plus 30 acres of fall plants and pumpkins.

The Rader family wants visitors to "harvest memories," and they succeed. Signs featuring a friendly scarecrow point the way to the food, corn mazes and attractions. Visitors set out with a map to locate the stations within the maze. Lost? Call the number on the map and the "corn cops" will find you!

It's easy to spend a few hours inside the activities area, which includes a straw castle, tire towers, corn kernel "sandboxes," pumpkin checkers and a huge jumping pillow made for bouncing. Visitors can shoot at targets with a corn blaster. Kids under 6 love the Little Village, where farm animals and equipment teach about country life. The farm also has a 1951 pickup truck for a photo op. We always stop for fresh cider.

Then it's on to the pumpkins! While they're already piled high for customers to easily browse and purchase, many folks prefer to pick their own, pulling a wagon into the pumpkin patch. Somehow these pumpkins seem more colorful—and much more memorable—than those lined up at our supermarket. Everyone is allowed as much time as needed to choose the perfect one.

Afterward, we buy decorative gourds and Indian corn. And sometimes a dozen pumpkin doughnuts and an apple pie find their way into the basket.

The temperature is cool by the time we head home, and the sun sets earlier. For us, a day at the corn maze and pumpkin patch truly means autumn has arrived. ☀

Clockwise from top left: Aerial view of the corn maze; a vintage truck decorated for fall; a scarecrow greets visitors who finish the maze; fun in the pumpkin patch.

Apples were key for many of Viola Shipman's (in middle) recipes.

The Pies with the 'S'

This grandmother created lasting inspiration from her kitchen.

BY WADE ROUSE

I spent a lot of time growing up in my grandma Viola's country kitchen, tugging at the hem of her ironed white aprons, each embroidered with bright strawberries or pretty flowers.

My tiny grandma and her little kitchen seemed larger than life to me as a child. A vintage stove anchored one side of the room, while her sparkly countertops were topped by a breadbox that held Little Debbies and Wonder Bread slices.

But the most prized possession in her kitchen was her recipe box. A brilliant baker, my grandma cherished the burnished wood box jammed with beloved and secret family recipes, organized into different categories—Pies, Cakes, Cookies, Breads—and all written in her slanting cursive.

Her Formica dinette table provided the glamorous backdrop for her glorious fresh fruit pies, mostly strawberry-rhubarb, blueberry, apple and cherry. The golden crusts were decorated with a pretty "S" for her last name, Shipman, the only demonstrable sign of pride my grandma ever presented.

Her cookies—chocolate chip, oatmeal and thumbprints filled with homemade jams—were devoured before they even had a chance to cool.

That tiny kitchen was not only the area where my family gathered every Sunday and holiday, but also where I learned to cook and bake, my grandma teaching me the history of our family through the food she made. Her kitchen wasn't just a place to cook; it was the place where she connected our family's past to the present.

Her kitchen is where I shared my life with her, too. After baking, she would always cut two slices of pie, pour a cup of coffee for herself and a glass of milk for me, and we'd sit and talk at her table. We'd mostly discuss what I was going to do when I grew up, how I was going to change the world and see places she never had the chance to see herself.

"What do you think Paris is like in the spring?" she'd ask. "Send me a postcard when you go."

I was still in college when my grandma hosted her last Thanksgiving. I returned home on break and spent most of my time in the kitchen with her, baking the pies for our family, decorating the tops with that signature "S." When we finished, she cut two slices and poured the coffee and milk, as always.

"Tell me about Chicago," she said, eyes wide, elbows resting on her Formica table.

Every Thanksgiving, I still make the treasured desserts from my grandma's recipe box. And after I finish, I still cut two slices of pie, pour a cup of coffee for her and a glass of milk for myself, take a seat at my own kitchen table, and tell my grandma all about my life. ☀

Every Thanksgiving, I still make the treasured desserts from my grandma's recipe box.

The bond young Wade shared with his grandmother continued to grow through the years.

Sowing Seeds of Hope

An injured soldier and his wife find healing on their Tennessee farm.

BY JILL GLEESON

United States Army Capt. Michael Trost almost died. It was Feb. 20, 2012, and Michael was serving in Spin Boldak, Afghanistan, as a civil affairs specialist, working with local communities to help build infrastructure. He and his team were escorting U.S. Agency for International Development representatives to a village in the southeastern region of the country when the group came under machine-gun fire.

Michael was hit five times and lost 12 units of blood before being taken by medevac to Kandahar, where he underwent the first of more than 30 surgeries to repair his wounded body.

Michael had lost most of one hand, including his index finger and thumb, and suffered wounds to his abdomen, legs and buttocks. The sciatic nerve in his right leg was severed, making it impossible initially for him to walk and causing excruciating pain that would last for several years, until his lower leg was amputated.

And yet, a half-decade later the 55-year-old and his wife, Stephanie, embarked on a physically demanding new adventure: farming 25 acres of land in Madisonville, Tennessee. They purchased the property, which is located 30 miles south of their Maryville home, in 2017. Soon after, they began working the land with the help of a backhoe donated through A Warrior's Wish, a program founded by a nonprofit veterans service organization called Hope for the Warriors.

"Whether it's trenching out lines or digging out areas for the equipment shed," Michael says of the machine, "it's just been a godsend. I don't know what I would have done without it. It's been an instrumental tool in helping me get this farm thing off the ground."

Michael has already put in an acre of organic hops, while Stephanie is installing organic vegetable beds. They've put up a chicken coop and a five-stall equipment shed, as well as 2,500 feet of fence. A greenhouse is on the way, and the pair are building a log cabin, which they plan to rent out through Airbnb and Farm Stay U.S. to help with the mortgage.

Asked how he went from surviving such grievous injuries to actually thriving, Michael, who retired from the military in 2014, replies, "I got through my toughest times with my faith in Jesus Christ, my beautiful wife and an inner determination my dad instilled in me to never quit."

A California native, Michael enlisted right out of high school, inspired by his father's career in the Marine Corps and by his great-uncles who fought in World War II. Michael spent 32 years in the Army, 20 of which were active duty, including a deployment to Mosul, Iraq, in 2004–'05. He is the recipient of numerous medals, among them a Purple Heart and a Bronze Star.

Michael and Stephanie, who have been married for more than a decade, moved to Maryville in 2008, where they set about converting the rural 7-acre parcel of land that surrounds their house into what Stephanie calls a hobby farm. It turned out to be great practice for their working farm in Madisonville.

"We built multiple barns and added horses, chickens and donkeys," Stephanie says. "We also had a big garden where we grew vegetables and put in an orchard. So we did a lot of farming stuff here on the property small-scale. We love it."

The couple's time in paradise was interrupted first by Michael's deployment to Afghanistan and then by his

From left: This backhoe from A Warrior's Wish helped launch Capt. Michael Trost's hops farm; Michael with comrades in Afghanistan. The man on the far right is Cpl. Robert Rose, who Michael says saved his life; the couple at a Yankees game, where Michael was presented an electric wheelchair.

From left: The Trosts' first Madisonville hops crop was planted in the spring of 2018; work continues on the log cabin at the Trosts' new farm.

injuries, which forced him to spend 10 months at Walter Reed National Military Medical Center in Bethesda, Maryland. Although surgeons were able to save Michael's right leg, because of complications he decided to have it amputated below the knee in April 2016. Nearly a year passed before he returned home, finally almost pain-free.

A fan of craft beer, Michael had been tinkering with the idea of farming hops since around the time of his first convalescence in 2013, when he decided to plant an experimental hops garden at the Maryville property.

Michael earned a certificate in professional brewing science from Knoxville's South College, but his education didn't end there. He and Stephanie are enrolled in the Arcadia Center for Sustainable Food and Agriculture's Veteran Farmer Program at Alexandria, Virginia. They make the 1,000-mile round-trip journey every month to participate in the program, where they study subjects ranging from soil management to crop rotation, and farm land that once belonged to George Washington. All of that knowledge will come in handy as they continue to work on their crop.

Their hop rhizomes produce vines that eventually reach 18 to 20 feet high. These woody tendrils are tied to a trellis system, and the flowers—which resemble pine cones—are harvested in early September. The plant

is then cut down to about a foot above ground level, where it will sprout again come spring.

Michael plans to sell the hops to commercial and home brewers, who use the oil from inside the flower to flavor their beer. But he calls his time tending the farm "more therapeutic than anything. It helps me get up in the morning because it gives me a sense of purpose, a mission. Those rhizomes need me to water them and fertilize them and take care of them. If I have a limitation or something I can't do, I just find ways to make it work. I tire a little bit more quickly these days, mainly because I'm getting older. It kind of catches up to you."

In addition to the backhoe, Michael gets help from a young Marine he's hired to assist him on the farm. Stephanie says she's seen how working the land has not only benefited her husband but also their farmhand.

"He struggles very badly with post-traumatic stress disorder," she says of their helper. "He's very antisocial. But he tells us every day, 'You don't know what you're doing for me. I can't tell you how this is helping me.' I think farming is very cathartic for vets because it's physically exhausting, but it's also about creating something, being part of something and having your hands in the dirt. There's something about just being out in the dirt that is healing." ☀

The Games of Fall

A flock of geese flying overhead proved that, in autumn, nature is the best playground.

BY WILMA J. WILLIAMS *Los Angeles, California*

Growing up in rural Arkansas, we watched for the geese as their annual caravan made its way through our neck of the woods. We knew they came from somewhere up north. We also knew they were headed to their winter destination, someplace down south.

Between September and November (when Canada geese migrate) it was still fairly warm in our parts. Because we were outdoor creatures, we stayed on the lookout for those friendly wings to come flapping our way high in the sky.

Back in the 1950s, many poor rural families didn't have a television to occupy their time. So every little thing that happened in nature was exciting to us, even the wind blowing up dust, leaves swirling through the autumn air, or storm clouds gathering on the horizon. Everything beyond our ordinary day-to-day activities was a big deal for us country kids.

Now here's how the "geese" thing goes. First, we had to be at home in order to see them. The only place that I remember seeing them fly over was at my house. While it appeared that divine providence charted their route slightly to the east of our house, I also had sense enough to know that our house just happened to be along their flight route.

If we were inside the house and somewhat quiet, we might hear their honking a little while before they came into view. But just in case we didn't hear them, whoever was in the yard and heard the first honk hollered, "Hey, y'all, the geese are coming!"

Then we bolted out of the house and fixed our eyes toward the eastern skies. And as if we thought the flight crew could hear us, we'd yell "hello!" and wave animatedly at them. We stood there flailing our arms until the winged creatures were long out of sight.

It's been a long time since I've seen the geese flying overhead. But each year around the time that they should be heading south, I turn on the camera in my mind, click "play," and I'm a skinny little country girl again, standing out in our front yard. ☀

MY COUNTRY MEMORY

TASTE OF THE COUNTRY

Cranberry Pecan Stuffing

PREP: 30 min. • **BAKE:** 40 min.
MAKES: 13 servings

- 1 **cup orange juice**
- ½ **cup dried cranberries**
- ½ **lb. bulk pork sausage**
- ¼ **cup butter, cubed**
- 3 **celery ribs, chopped**
- 1 **large onion, chopped**
- 1 **tsp. poultry seasoning**
- 6 **cups seasoned stuffing cubes**
- 1 **medium tart apple, peeled and finely chopped**
- ½ **cup chopped pecans**
- ¼ **tsp. salt**
- ⅛ **tsp. pepper**
- ¾ **to 1 cup chicken broth**

1. In a small saucepan, bring orange juice and cranberries to a boil. Remove from the heat; let stand for 5 minutes. Meanwhile, in a large skillet, cook the sausage until no longer pink; drain. Transfer to a large bowl.
2. In the same skillet, melt butter. Add celery and onion; saute until tender. Stir in poultry seasoning.
3. Add to the sausage mixture. Stir in the stuffing cubes, orange juice mixture, apple, pecans, salt, pepper and enough chicken broth to reach desired moistness.
4. Transfer to a greased 13x9-in. baking dish. Cover dish and bake at 325° for 30 minutes. Uncover; bake until lightly browned, 10-15 minutes longer.

¾ **cup:** 219 cal., 11g fat (4g sat. fat), 16mg chol., 532mg sod., 27g carb. (8g sugars, 2g fiber), 4g pro.

Caramel Pecan Pie

PREP: 25 min. • **BAKE:** 35 min. + cooling • **MAKES:** 8 servings

36	caramels
¼	cup water
¼	cup butter, cubed
3	large eggs, room temperature
¾	cup sugar
1	tsp. vanilla extract
⅛	tsp. salt
1⅓	cups chopped pecans, toasted
	Frozen deep-dish pie shell
	Pecan halves, optional

1. In a small heavy saucepan, combine caramels, water and butter. Cook and stir over low heat until caramels are melted. Remove from the heat and set aside.
2. In a small bowl, beat the eggs, sugar, vanilla and salt until smooth. Gradually add caramel mixture. Stir in chopped pecans. Pour into pie crust. If desired, arrange pecan halves over filling.
3. Bake at 350° for 35-40 minutes or until set. Cool on a wire rack. Refrigerate leftovers.

1 piece: 541 cal., 29g fat (7g sat. fat), 88mg chol., 301mg sod., 68g carb. (49g sugars, 2g fiber), 7g pro.

Citrus Rainbow Carrots

TAKES: 25 min. • **MAKES:** 6 servings

2	lbs. medium rainbow or regular carrots, diagonally sliced
3	Tbsp. butter
2	Tbsp. sugar
1½	tsp. grated orange zest
2	Tbsp. orange juice
¾	tsp. salt
¼	tsp. pepper
⅛	tsp. ground cloves

1. Place carrots and enough water to cover in a large saucepan; bring to a boil. Reduce heat; cook, uncovered, until tender, 8-10 minutes. Drain; return to pan.
2. Add the remaining ingredients. Cook over medium-high heat until the carrots are glazed, 2-3 minutes, stirring occasionally.

⅔ cup: 132 cal., 6g fat (4g sat. fat), 15mg chol., 445mg sod., 19g carb. (12g sugars, 4g fiber), 2g pro.

Savory Cheese Ball

PREP: 15 min. + chilling · **MAKES:** 2 cups

- 1　pkg. (8 oz.) cream cheese, softened
- 1　cup crumbled blue cheese
- ¼　cup butter, softened
- 1　can (4¼ oz.) chopped ripe olives
- 1　Tbsp. minced chives
- ¼　cup chopped walnuts
- 　　Assorted crackers

1. In a large bowl, beat the cream cheese, blue cheese and butter until smooth. Stir in olives and chives. Cover and refrigerate for at least 1 hour.

2. Shape cheese mixture into a ball; roll in walnuts. Wrap in plastic; refrigerate for at least 1 hour. Serve with crackers.

To make pumpkin shape: Using a knife, score vertical lines along the outside of the ball; insert a broccoli stem into the top.

2 Tbsp.: 120 cal., 12g fat (6g sat. fat), 28mg chol., 227mg sod., 1g carb. (0 sugars, 0 fiber), 3g pro.

Mini Pretzel Pumpkins

PREP: 30 min. + standing · **MAKES:** 2 dozen

- ½　lb. white candy coating, coarsely chopped
- 24　miniature pretzels
- 　　Orange-colored sugar or sprinkles
- 6　green gumdrops, each cut into 4 lengthwise slices

1. In a microwave, melt the candy coating; stir until smooth. Dip 1 pretzel in candy coating; let the excess drip off.

2. Place on waxed paper-lined baking sheet. If desired, fill the pretzel holes with candy coating. Decorate with orange sugar or sprinkles. For stem, dip the back of 1 gumdrop piece into candy coating; place above the pumpkin. Repeat. Let stand until set, about 30 minutes.

1 pumpkin: 61 cal., 3g fat (2g sat. fat), 0 chol., 27mg sod., 9g carb. (7g sugars, 0 fiber), 0 pro.

Classic Chili

PREP: 10 min. • **COOK:** 1 hour 50 min.
MAKES: 12 servings (3 qt.)

1	medium green pepper, chopped
2	medium onions, chopped
½	cup chopped celery
1	Tbsp. vegetable oil
2	lbs. ground beef
2	cans (28 oz. each) diced tomatoes, undrained
1	can (8 oz.) tomato sauce
1	cup water
2	Tbsp. Worcestershire sauce
1	to 2 Tbsp. chili powder
1	tsp. garlic powder
1	tsp. dried oregano
1	tsp. salt
½	tsp. pepper
2	cans (16 oz. each) kidney beans, rinsed and drained
	Tortilla chips, optional

In a Dutch oven or large soup kettle, saute green pepper, onions and celery in oil until tender, about 5 minutes. Add the ground beef and cook until browned; drain. Stir in the tomatoes, tomato sauce, water, Worcestershire sauce and seasonings. Bring to a boil; reduce heat. Cover and simmer for 1½ hours, stirring occasionally. Add kidney beans. Simmer, uncovered, 10 minutes longer. If desired, serve with tortilla chips.

1 cup: 259 cal., 10g fat (4g sat. fat), 47mg chol., 708mg sod., 23g carb. (7g sugars, 7g fiber), 20g pro.

Skillet Pork Chops with Apples & Onion

TAKES: 20 min. • **MAKES:** 4 servings

- 4 **boneless pork loin chops (6 oz. each)**
- 3 **medium apples, cut into wedges**
- 1 **large onion, cut into thin wedges**
- ¼ **cup water**
- ⅓ **cup balsamic vinaigrette**
- ½ **tsp. salt**
- ¼ **tsp. pepper**

1. Place a large nonstick skillet over medium heat; brown pork chops on both sides, about 4 minutes. Remove from pan.

2. In the same skillet, combine apples, onion and water. Place the pork chops over apple mixture; drizzle chops with vinaigrette. Sprinkle with salt and pepper. Reduce heat; simmer, covered, until a thermometer inserted in chops reads 145°, 3-5 minutes.

1 pork chop with ¾ cup apple mixture: 360 cal., 15g fat (4g sat. fat), 82mg chol., 545mg sod., 22g carb. (15g sugars, 3g fiber), 33g pro.
Diabetic exchanges: 5 lean meat, 1 fruit, 1 fat.

Stuffing Crust Turkey Potpie

PREP: 35 min. • **BAKE:** 20 min. • **MAKES:** 6 servings

2	cups cooked cornbread stuffing
3	to 4 Tbsp. chicken broth
2	oz. cream cheese, softened
½	cup turkey gravy
2	cups cubed cooked turkey
1	cup frozen broccoli florets, thawed
½	cup shredded Swiss cheese
¼	tsp. salt
¼	tsp. pepper
2	cups mashed potatoes
¼	cup half-and-half cream
2	Tbsp. butter, melted
½	cup french-fried onions, optional

1. Preheat oven to 350°. In a small bowl, combine the stuffing and enough broth to reach desired moistness; press onto the bottom and up the sides of a greased 9-in. deep-dish pie plate. Bake until lightly browned, 10-15 minutes.

2. In a large bowl, beat cream cheese and gravy until smooth. Stir in the turkey, broccoli, Swiss cheese, salt and pepper. Spoon over crust.

3. In a small bowl, combine potatoes and cream; spread over turkey mixture. Drizzle with butter. If desired, sprinkle with onions. Bake until heated through and lightly browned, 20-25 minutes.

1 piece: 389 cal., 20g fat (9g sat. fat), 73mg chol., 910mg sod., 30g carb. (2g sugars, 2g fiber), 22g pro.

Grandma's Biscuits

TAKES: 25 min. • **MAKES:** 10 biscuits

2	cups all-purpose flour
3	tsp. baking powder
1	tsp. salt
⅓	cup shortening
⅔	cup 2% milk
1	large egg, lightly beaten

1. Preheat oven to 450°. In a large bowl, whisk flour, baking powder and salt. Cut in the shortening until mixture resembles coarse crumbs. Add milk; stir just until moistened.

2. Turn onto a lightly floured surface; knead gently 8-10 times. Pat dough into a 10x4-in. rectangle. Cut rectangle lengthwise in half; cut crosswise to make 10 squares.

3. Place 1 in. apart on an ungreased baking sheet; brush the tops with egg. Bake until golden brown, 8-10 minutes. Serve warm.

1 biscuit: 165 cal., 7g fat (2g sat. fat), 20mg chol., 371mg sod., 20g carb. (1g sugars, 1g fiber), 4g pro.

HANDCRAFTED WITH LOVE

Pumpkin Cross-Stitch

Get ready for fall with a
sweet gourd design.

WHAT YOU'LL NEED

- DMC six-strand embroidery floss in
  colors listed on color key
- Scissors
- Tapestry needle
- 9-in. square 18-count Aida cloth in
  oatmeal
- 5½-in. embroidery hoop
- Cardboard

DIRECTIONS

1. Fold Aida cloth in half lengthwise
   and crosswise to find center.
2. Separate 2 strands of dark orange
   floss and cut to an 18-in. length.
   Thread needle and begin stitching
   at center. Each square on chart
   equals 1 stitch worked over
   2 Aida squares in each direction.
3. Continue stitching, changing colors
   according to chart, and working
   thread ends under stitches on back
   of piece.
4. When finished, center piece in
   hoop. Trim excess Aida cloth,
   leaving a 1-in. border.
5. Cut cardboard to fit inside small
   hoop circle on back. Work edges of
   cloth around the back of the hoop,
   and fit cardboard into hoop to
   secure edges in place.

COLOR KEY
Dark orange: 946
Light orange: 3853
Yellow: 725
Dark green: 3345
Light green: 581
Brown: 829
Maroon: 814

Beeswax Wrap

Give lunch and leftovers a pretty new cover.

WHAT YOU'LL NEED
- 12-in. square light cotton fabric
- Parchment paper
- ½ oz. beeswax
- Cookie sheet
- Box grater
- Paintbrush

DIRECTIONS
1. Spread fabric on a cookie sheet lined with parchment paper.
2. Grate beeswax onto fabric and spread evenly. Place in a preheated 300° oven until wax melts, about 2 minutes. Remove from oven and quickly spread any extra wax to dry areas of fabric, using a paintbrush. Hang to dry completely before using.

NOTE Wash by hand with cool water and dish soap. Wraps can be re-waxed when they lose their "cling," or they can be composted.

Seasonal Signage

Create a reversible set of wood blocks to welcome guests.

WHAT YOU'LL NEED
- 1x3x36-in. wood board
- Acrylic craft paint in variety of colors
- Saw
- Paintbrush
- Stencils of alphabet letters

DIRECTIONS
1. Cut board into three 3-in. lengths, two 6-in. lengths, one 7-in. length and one 7½-in. length.
2. Paint each block in preferred color scheme, alternating colors on blocks as desired. Dry thoroughly.
3. On 7-in. piece, in a coordinating color, stencil "W" on one side. Dry thoroughly and stencil "A" on the other side.
4. Repeat the process with the remaining blocks. On one 6-in. block, stencil "I" on one side and "U" on reverse, and on the second stencil "R" on one side and "N." On one 3-in. block, stencil "N" and "T," on second, stencil "T" and "U" and on third, stencil "E" and "M." Lay the 7½-in. piece horizontally; stencil "WISHES" on one side and "BLESSINGS" on the other. Dry all pieces thoroughly.
5. Arrange the pieces to spell "AUTUMN BLESSINGS" and "WINTER WISHES."

Winter

Snow blankets both land and barn
near Kalispell, Montana.
PHOTO BY CHUCK HANEY

THE GOOD LIFE

Keeping Busy on the Tree Farm

Nothing went as planned, but it was a day full of learning and adventures.

BY CHARITY KEITH *Southwest City, Missouri*

My family owns and runs the Ozark Valley Christmas Tree Farm in Southwest City, Missouri. Our farm has been around since 1866, and my children are now the seventh generation to live on this land. My parents own a farm next to ours where they run a corn maze and pumpkin patch every fall. Jon, my husband, and I help my parents on their farm and they help on ours. It's a good partnership.

We're busy all year, even if our trees aren't purchased until the holiday season. In January we have to clean up and take down the equipment we used during selling season. We spend February cutting the stumps out of the fields—they have to be cut off at ground level to prevent harmful bugs from making homes in them.

The planting starts in March by drilling holes in the ground with a tractor-mounted auger. We have good soil in these Ozark hills, but there's not enough of it around all the rocks! So we bring in buckets of soil from the river bottomland to pour into the holes along with our seedlings, to give the roots a fighting chance.

As soon as we finish planting, it's time to start mowing and spraying. We spray weed killer around the trees so they can grow without competition from grasses, and we periodically spray fungicide (and sometimes insecticide) on the trees to keep them nice and healthy. Our spring and summer is mostly spent repeating this activity.

By the time June rolls around, the trees need to be sheared. Scotch pines don't grow into that nice, neat, traditional Christmas tree shape on their own, so we have to shear them to correct the form.

October is when we start getting ready for our selling season. We decorate our barn, set up crafters and vendors in the gift shop, get the equipment out and prepare the hot chocolate machine.

Then we open for business the day after Thanksgiving and close Christmas Eve—or when we run out of trees, whichever happens first!

On a normal day, I am a checklist kind of gal. I love having my daily tasks on a notepad, ready to be crossed

Charity Keith had a day that went hilariously off the plan.

off upon completion. One day, though, not even the best checklist would've saved me.

Here's a behind-the-scenes look at my minute-by-minute activities getting the trees ready for Christmas on a day when everything just seemed to go wrong.

7:30 a.m. Drop off the boys at school, then drop off our daughter with my mom. This gives me six hours to spray fungicide on the Christmas trees. Productivity awaits!

8 a.m. I had decided to try to make my own fungicide out of copper sulfate and lime. This requires a specific type of sprayer to keep the ingredients mixed in the tank, so I spend the next hour helping my dad fix the sprayer. I use the term "helping" loosely. My actual contributions include handing him tools and nodding encouragingly.

9 a.m. Head off to the field. Six hours of work await!

9:20 a.m. Sadly, I leave the field after just 20 minutes with a clogged and useless sprayer. Deciding to fling my thrifty attempt to the wind, I plan to call our local farm supply co-op and order the more expensive, yet sprayer-friendly, liquid counterpart.

The Keith children show off their family's trees.

9:25 a.m. I leave my very dirty work clothes on the porch before I go inside to make the call. I feel very safe doing this since our farm is rather secluded in the holler.

9:27 a.m. When I call the local co-op, I get a recorded message—"All circuits are busy right now. Try again later." I recall a similar incident in an episode of *The Andy Griffith Show*, and silently ponder why this technological glitch was not eradicated about the time of the advent of color television.

9:35 a.m. I abandon my attempt to order from the co-op. Determined to get something accomplished, I decide to head outside to wash out the clogged sprayer.

9:37 a.m. Emerging from my house in my underwear in an attempt to retrieve my work clothes from the porch railing, I shock a car full of solicitors in the driveway.

9:38 a.m. I run back inside the house to hastily dress, then emerge to greet my smiling guests.

9:40 a.m. Since I am so dirty I politely decline to shake their hands. They visit Mom next and, I find out later, tell her they appreciate her kind smile, because her neighbors "were not very cheerful today."

10 a.m. I attempt to drive to the hydrant on the farm to wash the sprayer, but my plan is quickly thwarted. I lay my head on the steering wheel in utter dejection when I realize our John Deere Gator won't start.

10:30 a.m. Time to stroll to the barn. Get Dad, a truck and jumper cables. We get the Gator started. I ask my Uncle Gary, who is on the farm fixing one of our tractors,

to look at the Gator's innards to help identify which part is misbehaving.

Noon I sit down to eat lunch but don't have time for dessert. In retrospect, this is the worst mistake of the day.

12:45 p.m. I'm finally ready to make a third attempt to wash out the sprayer. And now there are two that need to be cleaned. The tasks on my list are multiplying faster than I can keep up.

2 p.m. Finally feeling victorious—I actually get a task accomplished by cleaning out two sprayers. I check the clock and notice that my six hours of planned productivity have dwindled to one.

2:10 p.m. I lose both sprayers out of the back of the improperly closed Gator bed. I lay my head on the steering wheel again, feeling down and mentally calculating how many Christmas trees I would need to sell to replace my far-flung equipment.

2:15 p.m. Abandoning all previous attempts at working in the tree fields, I change direction. I will mow grass. I am empowered! This is a task at which I am competent. I will prevail! I can begin as soon as the mower is greased.

2:30 p.m. It doesn't take long to discover that a grease fitting is missing from the mower deck. I take note that this has never happened to me before. I begin to tally the items that have broken, clogged and quit today at my hand. The result is staggering.

3:15 p.m. Quit farming for the day. I can't afford myself. Here's hoping tomorrow is more productive! ☀

Found in the Big Lost

Guided by fate, a southern couple braves a brutal Idaho winter to find their forever home.

BY DAWN McKNIGHT *Moore, Idaho*

Patrick and Dawn admire views of Big Lost Range with their son-in-law David.

My dear husband, Patrick, and I moved from southern Mississippi to central Idaho's Big Lost River Valley during one of the heaviest snowstorms and harshest winters in Idaho's recent history. It was 20 below zero when we moved into our unfinished home amid swirling, blowing snow.

The house didn't even have a front door, and on the third floor, where a window was missing, a pair of giant white barn owls had made a nest. On our first night in the house, those owls swooped from the top floor, flew past us and out the open door. We named our place White Owl Farm in honor of that encounter.

We knew we were going to make the Big Lost River Valley our home when we drove through the area on a vacation and fell in love with the land and the people. We sought property that included enough acreage to grow apples, plant a big garden and raise chickens and goats.

Patrick and I happened upon an unfinished house with just the right amount of land on the Big Lost River near the base of Mount Borah, Idaho's tallest mountain.

The real estate agent told us that the sellers shared our last name, and we knew it was fate. An initial visit to the property reinforced our belief. Patrick and I share the same birthdate and, when we saw our birthday etched in a concrete slab near the house, we knew the house was our forever home.

Every morning we wake up to the sight of towering mountains: the Lost River Range to the north and east, Pioneer and White Knob mountains to the south and west.

"Lost" refers to the Big Lost emptying into an aquifer rather than into another river. It flows just past our front yard, and it seems to be a migratory route for ducks and geese. The sunsets and moonrises are spectacular; the night sky fills with brilliant stars. The river also brings moose, elk and deer to our place nearly every day.

The Big Lost River Valley is rich in both history and geological magnificence, rivaling places like Yosemite and Yellowstone national parks. Long ago, the Shoshone-Bannock Tribes called this area home, as evidenced by

The Big Lost River flows past Dawn and Patrick's front yard.

pictographs on nearby canyon walls. Fur trappers, then miners settled into the area, followed by some cattle ranchers and sheepherders.

We consider ourselves modern pioneers, and we had growing pains that first winter. When our truck wouldn't work, we learned about diesel fuel gelling. Our well and septic systems froze, and then, within days of our arrival, ice damming caused the Big Lost River to flood much of our property.

With his-and-hers shovels, we dug vehicles out of the snow. We piled thermals, wool hats, thick gloves and heavy snow boots next to the front door when they were not in use. Still, we had much to celebrate that icy first Christmas Day.

Winter is long and spring arrives late in Idaho. We had to wait on building and gardening, but as soon as the river began to flow and we could stick a shovel in the ground, we erected our greenhouse and prepared the soil for cultivation. We planted 30 apple trees and a garden, and ordered a beehive.

Then, the record snowpack in the mountains above us began to thaw. We were forced to stop working on the house to build a berm and to stack sandbags just in case the river flooded.

After two months, during which we watched the rising river and plugged holes in the barrier, the snow stopped melting in late July and we could focus on gardening and finishing the house.

We were blessed with a bounty of potatoes, lettuce, tomatoes, squash, carrots and onions from our garden despite a June snowfall. As summer wound down and the snowmelt diminished, the river flow slowed to a trickle as its water disappeared down into the Snake River Aquifer.

Fall comes early in the Big Lost, which means we started preparing for winter in August. We made many trips into the Sawtooth National Forest to gather wood for our wood stove, our main source of heat.

The bitter cold weather begins in September and hangs on through June, and we've been told we will need at least 10 cords of seasoned fuel to make it through.

The firewood-gathering trips, although hard work, have been great fun. We enjoy spectacular scenery and wildlife, and we often find a special rock or gem.

As if the river and high desert mountains weren't enchanting enough, our home sat in the direct path of the 2017 total solar eclipse. Friends and family joined us for the historic event. Many of them left our place with the hope of one day making the Big Lost River Valley their own forever home, too.

Moving from a warm climate to a cold one has been a challenge, but there is no place we'd rather be, especially during the holiday season. We ride out into the forest and cut down our tree. Families can obtain a tree-cutting permit, which makes the holidays feel old-fashioned.

Our grandchildren help make ornaments from things we have found in nature. And we make most of our gifts by hand: dolls, dollhouses, stuffed toys, and canned goods from the garden.

We dug an ice skating rink, and in winter we will play hockey with friends and family. Rose, our Great Pyrenees, will pull us on a sled, and we will build many snowmen. And while winter may be our favorite time of year, no matter the season, we can always be found in the Big Lost. ☀

From left: Daughter Amy gives her daughter McKenna a snowy ride;
Lucian loves to explore all around Grandma and Grandpa's land.

Where We're Supposed to Be

When the flurry of branding day is done,
there's time to pause and reflect on life in the country.

BY KATIE MARCHETTI *Bozeman, Montana*

The Asa Porter Ranch has been stewarded by the same family for six generations.

The ranch sits in the midst of the coastal hills in San Luis Obispo County, California.

On a Saturday in late February, when the grass starts growing rich and fiercely green, I walk around to the back of an old ranch house to a yard full of picnic tables for a barbecue. Folks in dirty jeans sit side by side on bench seats, and cowboy hats and sunglasses obscure faces as the hum of conversation and laughter rises up. Old trees stand sentinel nearby, bearing witness to the gathering.

This isn't my home, but it feels like it. At the Asa Porter Ranch in San Luis Obispo County, California, weathered barns and drifting cattle are the backdrop to tables laden with food as the late afternoon sun reflects off the cans held in tired, callused hands. John Porter and members of his family scoot down and make room, thanking me for making time to come by and eat their food. And I wonder if this style of generosity, this easy kindness, grows best here in the fertile California soil alongside alfalfa fields, under the Spanish moss, romanticizing the brittle branches of drought tolerant trees. It's where friends and strangers alike come early for a hard day's work and where a meal is payment enough. Before "pay it forward" was a trending hashtag on social media, it was lived out here for a hundred years or more.

A cute German shorthaired pointer wanders nearby, inquiring around the table legs and the scuffed boots, nudging the elbows of strangers for a pat on the head. Between bites of food, rookies tell of mistakes from the morning in the branding pen, of cold irons and shots misplaced. The experienced ranchers nod and say they "did a fine job" on the approximately 125 head of cattle branded that day, and they smile at their plates, the newly proud cowboys and the worn-out teachers.

When I first walk into the beautiful ranch house, I immediately notice glowing banisters and hardwood floors worn smooth by time. Faded wallpaper creates a muted backdrop for rows of black-and-white photos that tell a story of lives lived here, generations lined up in proud succession. I recognize them, although the faces and names of the Porter family are new to me, because they're hardworking, family-oriented, generous and steadfast people. I've seen photos like these treasured and displayed in homes around the country—the stoic and the joyful, posed in gentle focus, with an undercurrent of pride and satisfaction in a job well done, of things overcome, radiating in vivid clarity.

The sun pours through the kitchen window onto the women who are moving in a time-honored rhythm in the house on this branding day, swatting kids as they pass while chatting over tops of heads. The extended network of Porter women works with efficiency equal to their male counterparts, never seeing it as less important, this job of feeding and filling, rewarding and restoring the worn-out bodies. There's pride in this necessity—there's art and heart in filling a table, which never goes unappreciated by the hungry crowds milling just beyond the kitchen screen door.

When I head outside and walk down the dirt road, the sounds of the barbecue dim with each step. Barn doors swing on newly oiled hinges; sunlight blooms golden through the boards and bathes everything in a musty warmth. Tractors and trucks are lined up neatly, and the dust, chips and rust show the hours of use they've all withstood together.

I linger to hear conversations about repairs and water tanks, leases and wildlife, and cattle known by notches and tags. Leaning on a board fence, I watch the bulls—the feisty and the mellow eyeing each other as they mull over their new bachelor corral accommodations, one of the results of the day's work.

I notice a marked steadiness as well as kindness out here, and it seems those are qualities that grow dim when places like this recede in the rearview mirror. As dust billows behind a truck on the lane, I turn to the sun, breathing deeply and realizing there's no questioning that this is where we're supposed to be now. I'll never believe that heaven could be anything other than this: sleek cattle on rolling hills blanketed by new grass, the murmur of water bubbling over rocks in the river, and a meal under the oak trees after a hard day's work. ☀

The Porter family works to rope a calf—one of the 125 head of cattle on their ranch.

Amber's husband, Brady, leads the family home after their annual Christmas tree hunt in Wyoming's Bridger-Teton National Forest.

The Perfect Tree

An annual tradition yields quality family time.

BY AMBER ESPLIN *Fairview, Wyoming*

Every year my husband, Brady, our four boys and I head up the mountains in Bridger-Teton National Forest to pick out our Christmas tree (with a permit in hand). The air is fresh, and the solitude out there is just exhilarating.

Typically, we spend about an hour searching for the fullest, straightest tree. We inspect each snow-flocked spruce or pine in passing, searching for the complement to our farmhouse. I like to get one that's taller than I need, so I can cut off the lower branches and use them to make wreaths and garland.

My little ones sing "Jingle Bells"—and we all sing loudly without fear of bothering an audience.

It's traditions like this that bring us so much joy around Christmastime and help us realize what is really important. ☀

CAPTURE THE BEAUTY AROUND YOU

SCRAPBOOK

My husband built new doghouses for our basset hounds as a Christmas gift, and I added festive decorations.
MACKY LINEBERRY *Pierce, Idaho*

We had guests stay for a few days at our remote lodge. They planned to watch fireworks on New Year's Eve in Anchorage, but nature had other plans. A storm rolled in, and once the sky cleared a stunning show took place.
JOSEPH BRAMANTE *Palmer, Alaska*

While I was cleaning out the feed troughs, my daughter Trinity insisted on pulling her brother Tate around.
SHAYE COBB *Blairsville, Georgia*

My elf is 60 years old—a gift from Mom—and a tufted titmouse loves to visit him in the winter.
NANCY TULLY *East Stroudsburg, Pennsylvania*

My wife, Jeanette, went sledding with our grandkids Silas and Faith in Old Fort, North Carolina.
NICK KRANTZ *Stanwood, Washington*

Seven-year-old Hannah seemed fascinated by the first snowflakes of the season at Olympic National Park. It's a winter wonderland for kids.
DAVE LOGAN *Port Angeles, Washington*

At the Bar Horseshoe Ranch in Mackay, Idaho, an old farm wagon stands glowing at the foot of the Lost River Range. These mountains, part of the Rockies, are the tallest in Idaho.
PHOTO BY DAVID R. STOECKLEIN

Peach, Hazel, Betty, Pearl, Red, Louise, Delilah, Amelia, Cinnamon and Sugar wish you a Merry Christmas!
AMANDA STICE *Otterville, Missouri*

This is my John Deere 450G dozer with a six-way blade after a storm hit us with 42 inches of snow!
ROBERT FISHER *Burlington, West Virginia*

It looks as if this house finch is taking a snow shower under a dried-up sunflower.
NORMA LARRABEE GABRIEL *Menomonie, Wisconsin*

After an ice storm, the sun came out and cast the most beautiful bright glow on the trees in our backyard.
CHRISTINA RUTTER
Martinsburg, West Virginia

A covered bridge spans the frozen Amnicon River at Amnicon Falls State Park in South Range, Wisconsin.
KELLY JOHNSON *Eau Claire, Wisconsin*

I watched as our horses chased each other around the pasture in the cold, powdery snow.
JESSICA WAGNER *Versailles, Ohio*

Gus, our border collie puppy, sits on my quarter horse mare, Tazzi, at Snake River in Hells Canyon.
AMBER ANDERSON *Cottonwood, Idaho*

Cousins Braxton and Emma look at the lights outside on a snowy Christmas night.
DRUSILLA DYE *Alzada, Montana*

Our 6-year-old son, John Clayton, loves playing in the snow with his dog, Sugar.
SARA ROGERS *Coxs Creek, Kentucky*

I spotted the ewes looking out on a winter day, with a little lamb sneaking a peek, too.
ERIKA MILLER *Monroeville, Ohio*

My father is a second-generation farmer, and for more than 60 years he has looked over this land.
DANA DUSTERHOFT *Rocky Rapids, Alberta*

Pets make the holiday season happier! Every time I look at this picture
of my friend's dog Bailey, I get so excited for Christmas.
KRISTIN CROSBY *Rapid City, South Dakota*

**Christmas on the ranch means rosy cheeks, fuzzy horses, and time with family and friends.
This picture of my daughter Emily captures the spirit of the season.**
DANIELLE OTIS *Sandpoint, Idaho*

While visiting New Hampshire for the holidays, snow fell the night before. I couldn't resist capturing the scene.
PAUL JARVIS *Helena, Alabama*

My mom, Ethel, and my boyfriend, Mitch, pose with Mom's little Christmas tree.
CAROL KOROLUK *Endeavour, Saskatchewan*

This barred owl looked so majestic and peaceful while sitting in the snowy tree.
SARAH WENTZEL *Hines, Minnesota*

Even the snowmen sport holiday lights outside this former farm near Oakbank, Manitoba.
PHOTO BY DAVE REEDE PHOTOGRAPHY

We are a military family that used to live in Georgia and Hawaii. My son Jackson now loves playing in the snow up in the mountains.
AIMEE STEIMER *Oak Harbor, Washington*

I had so much fun watching the antics of these blue jays as they fought over the peanuts at my feeder.
MARY HINDLE *Ottawa, Ontario*

After a storm dropped a foot of snow on our farmette, my daughter Alayna, 8, and son Logan, 3, went for a stroll with the cat.
DARLENE SHIRK *Fleetwood, Pennsylvania*

A Teachable Tractor

*This boy is learning valuable lessons thanks to his dad
and his Pappy—and a little help from Santa.*

BY KEITH DOERSOM *Newville, Pennsylvania*

Our 1957 Farmall Cub was a gift for my son, Levi. I found it online in 2016, and Santa helped get it home for Christmas. Levi, who is 10, loves his Cub. It seems not a day goes by that he isn't on it.

It had been sitting for a number of years, so we've had to do some work on it. We overhauled the carburetor to clean out years of varnish and clogged passageways, and that got it running. After a while the charging system felt questionable so we installed a new voltage regulator and overhauled the generator. We stuck with the 6-volt system—it worked for 60 years, it'll work for 60 more. A few months later the Cub developed four stuck exhaust valves, but after a complete valve job, it ran well.

The Farmall has taught my son valuable mechanical skills. He devours books on tractors and asks thoughtful questions about them. We live on the family homestead, so he's learned much of what he knows from Pappy, his grandfather, and me (though at times I think he knows more about tractors than we do).

Levi enjoys taking the Cub to both tractor shows and parades. One Memorial Day he entered it in the local parade to honor his Great-Uncle Sam, who was killed in action in Vietnam. He also takes his mother, his dog and me for rides around the block in the wagon we built. The Cub gets him out of the house and ensures he's not in front of screens all day.

Levi's goal is to farm and have a landscape business. I grew up helping family members on their farms, and the lessons I learned—responsibility; respect for machinery; and love, respect and compassion for family, friends and animals—can't be taught many other ways.

While we don't have a farm, we are fortunate to have 20 acres of woods that allow my wife and me to raise our son in the same way we grew up. The only thing he's missing is the joy of baling hay on a 100-degree day. ☀

When it snows, Levi loves to start the Cub and get to work.

Grandma's bread was more precious than any toy or treat.

Home-Baked Happiness

The recipe for the perfect present mixes Grandma's love with a dash of heritage.

BY RICHARD PIERCE *Pingree Grove, Illinois*

In the early 1900s, Marie Hasselbusch, my grandmother, and her sister Lena traveled from Germany to America. They were two adventurous and brave teenagers leaving their family behind for a brighter future.

Once in America, they started to build their lives in this country. My grandmother married William Witte, who also came here from Germany. They had four daughters and a son. My mother, Lillian, was the oldest.

My grandfather worked as a stair builder, and he constructed a home from scratch on Chicago's west side.

They lived in that house for the rest of their lives.

Their five children went on to have their own families, blessing Grandma and Grandpa with a total of 21 grandkids! I am the oldest, so I watched our huge family grow.

My grandmother always insisted on giving Christmas presents to every grandchild. On Christmas Eve you could hardly enter their bungalow because of the packages. They were not expensive, but rather simple gifts from the heart such as gloves and crayons.

Even so, once more and then more grandchildren arrived, gift-giving became a challenge for Grandma and Grandpa. So one year when I was still a teenager, I told my grandmother that I really didn't need to get a gift for Christmas.

But she insisted, and I told her, "Just give me a loaf of your bread."

When Grandma came over from Germany as a girl, she didn't bring many possessions along with her—but she remembered how her mother baked bread.

For as long as I can remember, Grandma baked several loaves of bread almost every week. You could tell when she was making bread by the tempting aroma coming from her kitchen as you walked up to their house.

She would set tins of dough in the bedrooms to rise. The smells and the sight of her making the bread are memories I'll never forget. She baked with wheat and white flour, and it was delicious!

Every year on Christmas Eve, Grandma and Grandpa sang an emotional "O Tannenbaum" in their native German, and then we opened our presents. My gift that year was indeed a loaf of my grandmother's bread. It was such a cherished part of her history, and that made it so special to me. ☀

Santa Made a Mistake

Sometimes the greatest gifts aren't found under the tree.

BY MARYANN K. NUNNALLY *Wilmington, North Carolina*

The winter that I turned 6 and my brother turned 5, Mom made it very clear that Christmas would be sparing on our farm in upstate New York. It was 1942 and a world war was being fought.

"Santa Claus has to give gifts to many children, so you should not be greedy," she said. "When you write your letter to Santa, you must only ask for one gift each."

That didn't seem too bad to me because all I wanted was a baby doll, and Wally really wanted a wheelbarrow. We didn't know that we were poor, but we understood there wasn't any extra money for toys and frivolities.

So on Christmas morning we were both delighted to find just what we wanted under the tree. My doll was dressed in a pink and white gingham dress and bonnet made from the material Mom had used to make my Sunday dress. I thought Santa was very clever to have picked out a dress just like mine, as my doll and I would look truly splendid in our matching outfits.

Wally's miniature bright red wheelbarrow came with a set of child-sized garden tools, including a rake, hoe and shovel. All that Christmas Day, he pretended to be a farmer with a garden and a field of crops to tend to.

Happily, I played with my doll using an old shoebox as a baby bed. With a string tied through the hole that Dad punched in the box, I managed to pull her around. But I had my eye on his wheelbarrow. It was the perfect size to lay my doll in and wheel her around the house.

When Wally left to help Dad in the barn, I wrapped my doll in her blanket and placed her in his wheelbarrow.

All was well until Wally returned to the house. He took one look at how I was using the wheelbarrow and tipped my doll out onto the floor. Giving me an angry scowl, he stomped off with the wheelbarrow.

So I had to settle for the shoebox. Several days later my father told me to help him sweep out the barn after breakfast. I was just thrilled! Usually Wally got to help Dad while I stayed inside to help Mom around the house.

In the barn, Dad handed me the push broom and then showed me where to sweep. I knew how to clean up all the small pieces of sawdust and hay that had accumulated on the floor, and I soon had a nice pile of odds and ends.

When I called Dad to inspect what I had done, he patted my head and said, "Good work, but you missed that junk over in the corner." What I found was an irregular bundle wrapped in brown paper and tied with string.

"Please, get that mess out of here," Dad said.

I pulled the package from the corner. On the top in black letters were the words, "For Maryann, from Santa Claus." Pointing to the message, I asked my dad, "Is this for me?"

"Sure looks like it," he said. "Why don't you open it?" Using the jackknife that he always carried, he cut the string holding the brown paper together.

And there it was, another little red wheelbarrow!

"Goofy Santa Claus must have left your wheelbarrow out here in the barn!" Dad said. "Well, now you have your very own wheelbarrow to put the baby in. And now your mother will expect you to use it to help her in the garden."

I tried to say something, but I could only stand there holding the gift. Finally, I said, "Can I please go back to the house?"

Dad nodded, buttoned my coat, tied my scarf and sent me back to the house to wheel my baby doll around in pure, absolute happiness.

There have been many Christmases since, but none can ever compare to the one when Santa Claus made a mistake.

Years later on a snowy December day at my father's funeral, I asked my mother where the Christmas wheelbarrow had come from. Mom explained that Dad had made a trip into the city to get it for me. She added, "We did not have the money for things like that, but your dad insisted. He loved you so much and never wanted you to go without." ☀

Minnesota's heavy snow is no match for John and his shovel.

Dad vs. the Driveway

There's nothing like the thrill of conquering winter's worst,
one scoop of snow at a time.

BY JOHN RABAEY *Marshall, Minnesota*

Early one Monday in January 2007, when a foot of snow had fallen overnight and the temperature had plummeted to minus 10, I was initiated into the routine familiar to generations of Minnesota settlers.

"Morning." My dad, also named John, stated a fact that was not obvious, given the darkness. "We need to clear the driveway. I have to be at work in two hours."

Dad grew up on a Minnesota farm, shoveling grain, feeding cattle, walking beans, picking rocks and driving tractors. He did not believe in snowblowers. He still fought the snow with a shovel.

Though annoyed, I dutifully got out of bed and dressed in layer after layer: underwear, shirt, socks, sweatpants, sweatshirt, snowpants, coat, boots, face mask, gloves and stocking cap. I braced myself, opened the door, and nearly fell over from the icy wind.

The driveway, short by farm standards but long to a 7-year-old kid with a shovel, was covered by hard-packed drifts. A snowplow had already cleared the county road, tossing a huge heap of snow onto the mouth of the driveway, and Dad was out there busily demolishing it.

He showed me how to attack the snow: Clear a long aisle down the center, then walk sideways down the aisle, taking quick scoops as you go. If you stop moving, you'll lose momentum. If the snow is too deep, take off 6 inches at a time; when you reach the end of the aisle, turn around and come back.

I tried, but I was a hopeless case. The shovel was too big for me and I couldn't manage the weight. While I struggled, Dad conquered the driveway in record time. I think it was the satisfaction of winning this fight that kept him from buying a snowblower—not the financial constraints he mentioned when my mom, Jennifer, brought it up.

Dad loves battling the elements. He enjoys the burn in his muscles, the adrenaline in his veins, the pumping of his heart. He handed down this love to all six of his sons. Even though he eventually bought a tractor that clears the yard in minutes, he often makes us shovel by hand, for the sheer joy of it.

Over the years, like Dad, I have come to relish the annual combat with the Minnesota snow. It gets my blood pumping and wakes me up. Plus it's a great excuse to get out in the crisp winter air. ☀

Message on the Horizon

One family found a unique way to display their faith.

BY DICK SHOUER *Freeport, Illinois*

If you should happen to be cruising along a stretch of U.S. Highway 20 a few miles east of Ridott, Illinois, a certain red barn can't help but catch your eye. Green and white shingles on its roof spell out in bold letters: "TO GOD BE THE GLORY."

A friend asked me to look into the barn's history to find out who had put those words on the roof.

The barn was built in 1915, but our story began in June 1972. Owner Gilbert Crull's sons—Steve, Jeff and Terry—were home from college for summer vacation, and that barn was in dire need of new shingles.

"I told the boys that a new roof on our barn had the potential to become a huge witnessing billboard," Gilbert said. "All they had to do was figure out a way to interlay the shingles in contrasting colors to read 'TO GOD BE THE GLORY.'"

Steve, a math major, took charge of the project. So the sign would be seen from a distance, he calculated the largest letters they could use and cut stencils to ensure they'd fit. White shingles against a background of green formed the words.

"You'll note the barn is positioned on a rise at a slight angle to the road," Steve told me. "This really enhances its visibility to people as they drive by. To me, these words provide a unique testimony regarding who is really in charge of our lives."

Over the years, the old barn has become an unofficial Stephenson County landmark and legend. It survived a violent rainstorm in August 1965 when tornado-force winds swept through northwest Illinois heading east toward Pecatonica. The Crull barn stood directly in the path. Trees were uprooted, the electrical and telephone service disrupted; mobile homes were overturned and several barns flattened along the way.

Freeport's police chief said it was the most violent storm the county had seen in his lifetime. But while a concrete silo close by was demolished, miraculously, the old barn was spared.

A while back, I stopped to see the barn again, and I talked to Ken Heeren, its current owner. An online friend and over-the-road truck driver had asked him where his home was located. He gave his "billboard" barn on Highway 20 as a reference. The trucker said, "Why Ken, I know exactly where that is. I've driven by that barn and seen its message many times." ☀

From Grandma to Table

A spoon and platter bring back fond memories of her grandmother's delicious cooking.

BY MICHELLE HOYT *Pillsbury, North Dakota*

Maybe it was my son having his 30th birthday recently, but I started getting sentimental thoughts about family and the past, particularly about two simple items: a spoon and a platter. They're not expensive, rare, fancy or valuable, except to me.

The spoon and platter originally belonged to my maternal grandmother, Luella Olsen. When Mom asked me which of Grandma's heirlooms I would like to have someday, these were the two things I picked because I remembered her using them when I was growing up.

Grandma used this spoon to stir cookie dough. When she asked what I wanted for Christmas, she was thrilled when I'd say her date cookies and sugar cookies. They were the best cookies I have ever eaten. I know she used the spoon for other things, too, but I fondly remember those cookies.

It is a wonderful, sturdy spoon—strong just like Grandma was. Now I use it when I make my own homemade cookies. It makes me smile to take it out of the drawer and hold it in my hand, because it helps me remember her.

The heavy-duty platter is simple and plain, not ornate. This was Grandma's meat platter; any and all meat she prepared went on this dish. I still miss the way that woman could fry side pork, a very tasty cut of meat from next to the belly.

Dinner was never served from the frying pan or stove—the platter was placed on the table for the family to share from. She used to make gravy with the pan drippings and serve it with mashed potatoes and a lot of dumplings.

Just like the spoon, using the platter reminds me of Grandma. She was a simple lady who grew up during hard times, but she was always generous with everyone. Grandma shared from her table, from her kitchen and her life. I use the dish as my very own meat platter and treasure the memories.

For the first three years after we moved into this house I smelled side pork in the kitchen, even though I haven't had it in years. The sensation tugged at my heart.

I always wonder if Grandma was here watching us get settled in our new home and keeping an eye on us. The smell eventually faded away. But the platter and spoon are still here, helping me feel a connection to my past. ☀

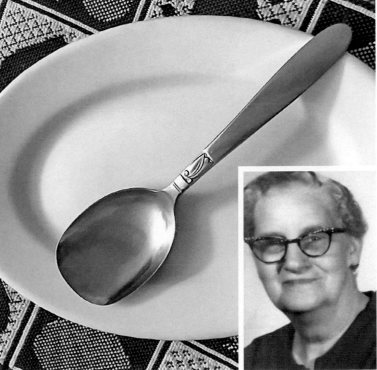

Michelle feels a special bond with Grandma Luella (inset) when she uses her kitchen tools.

A Nativity to Remember

Her husband hand-crafted a creche with love from the farm.

BY MARY ANN KOONTZ *Fort Wayne, Indiana*

Tom made this creche in 1980.

Christmas is a time for celebrating our faith and families, putting up decorations, and sharing memories and traditions from days gone by. All these things are wrapped up like Baby Jesus in our cherished creche, the one my husband, Tom, made using materials from his grandparents' woods.

Tom's late grandparents had lived just outside of Fort Wayne, Indiana, on a farm they named Walnut Hills. It was a special place to Tom because as a boy he, his brother and cousin spent a couple of weeks there each summer.

The children learned what real country life was all about—baling the hay and straw; feeding chickens, pigs and cows; and mucking out the animals' stalls.

Not everything was work, though. When chores were done, they found ample time to play in the woods. They built treehouses and fished in the creek that curled through the shade of walnut, hickory and maple trees.

A hill at the edge of the woods was perfect for trying out go-karts they built using scrap wood and tires found in the weathered barn.

It was a thrill to drive the tractor, mowing the main grassy trail that snaked through the woods. The trail ended at an old oak tree, its bent limbs pointing to open fields at the back of the property.

In the fall, the family chopped firewood to fuel the coal-burning furnace in the small farmhouse, which was built in the early 1900s.

In the winter they went skating on the frozen creek and sledded on the same hill that their go-karts had christened in the summer. Aboard snowmobiles, they raced along the snow-covered paths and out to the glistening fields.

Maybe it was because of these great memories that Tom chose pieces of bark and branches from those very woods to create a one-of-a-kind Nativity stable in 1980, the year our first child was born. He made all the pillars from cut branches, covering the roof with pieces of bark carefully arranged in an overlapping pattern.

On the back of the creche Tom added a music box that plays "Silent Night." Our two kids loved winding up the box on Christmas when they were young. A night light illuminates the creche's interior along with some figurines I stained and place in and around the Nativity scene each year.

As special Christmas gifts, Tom and I made Nativity sets for his grandparents, parents, brother and sister with wood from the farm, so they mean even more.

Every Christmas we carefully place our creche on a bed of cotton batting for display. The sight of it always transports Tom back to his childhood, and he relives the many fond memories he made at Walnut Hills farm. ☀

A light casts a holy glow on Tom and Mary Ann's creche.

The farmhouse in 1947; Grandma (in plaid skirt) and friends play in winter.

Footprints on the Farm

A walk back in time revealed the land where her grandma experienced happy moments.

BY KERYSA FORD *Ooltewah, Tennessee*

Last fall, for the first time, I visited the farm in Newmarket, New Hampshire, where my grandma Martha (Knowles) Ford grew up. She passed away several years ago, but during our time together she told me amazing stories. I couldn't wait to see her home for myself.

My great-grandfather Malcolm Knowles owned and farmed the land. The barn and house burned down in 1967, before I was born, and the farm was sold. The property is now preserved as part of the Tuttle Swamp Conservation Area.

I have a picture of the farmhouse taken after a heavy New England snowfall in 1947. Several of the large maple trees in front are still standing. They provided precious shade, where kids could play and swing. My great-grandfather likely tapped them for sugaring; his sugarhouse is one of few buildings remaining. I also cherish a photo of my grandma and some friends near the farm, taken during winter a few years earlier.

Grandma certainly didn't lack a sense of humor. One of my favorite stories was about an unwanted guest. She had found a squirmy "friend" somewhere outside and put it in her pocket for safekeeping. Taking it out at the table, of all places, she tossed it onto her father's plate. He was none too pleased to have a garter snake join him for dinner!

Upon walking the property last fall, I found small fragments of porcelain, remnants of farm equipment, and my personal favorite, a license plate from 1947. They were little reminders of the life that once flourished on this beautiful land when it was a working farm, complete with cows, chickens, horses, dogs, cats, fruit trees and an abundant garden.

I never got to see the farm in its prime, but it was so wonderful to walk the land and know that it will be preserved for future generations. ☀

Gingerbread Cutout Cookies

PREP: 30 min. + chilling
BAKE: 10 min./batch + cooling
MAKES: 5 dozen

- ¾ cup butter, softened
- 1 cup packed brown sugar
- 1 large egg, room temperature
- ¾ cup molasses
- 4 cups all-purpose flour
- 2 tsp. ground ginger
- 1½ tsp. baking soda
- 1½ tsp. ground cinnamon
- ¾ tsp. ground cloves
- ¼ tsp. salt

    Vanilla frosting of your choice

    Red and green paste food coloring

1. In a large bowl, cream butter and brown sugar until light and fluffy. Add egg and molasses. Combine the flour, ginger, baking soda, cinnamon, cloves and salt; gradually add to creamed mixture and mix well. Cover dough and refrigerate until easy to handle, about 4 hours or overnight.

2. Preheat oven to 350°. On a lightly floured surface, roll the dough to ⅛-in. thickness. Cut with floured 2½-in. cookie cutters. Place 1 in. apart on ungreased baking sheets.

3. Bake until the edges are firm, 8-10 minutes. Remove to wire racks to cool. Tint some of the frosting red and some green; leave remaining frosting plain. Decorate cookies.

1 cookie: 77 cal., 2g fat (1g sat. fat), 10mg chol., 69mg sod., 13g carb. (6g sugars, 0 fiber), 1g pro.

Roasted Brussels Sprouts with Cranberries

PREP: 15 min. • **BAKE:** 20 min. • **MAKES:** 12 servings

- 3 lbs. fresh Brussels sprouts, trimmed and halved
- 3 Tbsp. olive oil
- 1 tsp. kosher salt
- ½ tsp. pepper
- ½ cup dried cranberries

Preheat oven to 425°. Divide Brussels sprouts between 2 greased 15x10x1-in. baking pans. Drizzle with oil; sprinkle with salt and pepper. Roast until tender, 20-25 minutes. Transfer to bowl; stir in cranberries.

½ cup: 94 cal., 4g fat (1g sat. fat), 0 chol., 185mg sod., 14g carb. (6g sugars, 5g fiber), 4g pro.
Diabetic exchanges: 1 vegetable, 1 fat.

Red Velvet Cinnamon Rolls

PREP: 20 min. + rising • **BAKE:** 15 min. • **MAKES:** 12 servings

- 1 pkg. red velvet cake mix (regular size)
- 2½ to 3 cups all-purpose flour
- 1 pkg. (¼ oz.) active dry yeast
- 1¼ cups warm water (120° to 130°)
- ½ cup packed brown sugar
- 1 tsp. ground cinnamon
- ¼ cup butter, melted

ICING
- 2 cups confectioners' sugar
- 2 Tbsp. butter, softened
- 1 tsp. vanilla extract
- 3 to 5 Tbsp. 2% milk

1. Combine the cake mix, 1 cup flour and yeast. Add water; beat on medium speed 2 minutes. Stir in enough remaining flour to form a soft, sticky dough. Turn onto a floured surface; knead gently 6-8 times. Place in a greased bowl, turning once to grease the top. Cover; let rise until doubled, 2 hours. Meanwhile, in another bowl, mix brown sugar and cinnamon.
2. Punch down dough. Turn onto a floured surface; roll into a 18x10-in. rectangle. Brush with butter to within ¼ in. of edges; sprinkle with sugar mixture.
3. Roll up, starting with a long side; pinch seam to seal. Cut into 12 slices. Place cut sides up in a greased 13x9-in. baking pan. Cover; let rise until almost doubled, 1 hour.
4. Preheat oven to 350°. Bake until puffed and light brown, 15-20 minutes. Cool slightly.
5. Beat the confectioners' sugar, butter, vanilla and enough milk to reach a drizzling consistency. Drizzle icing over warm rolls.

1 cinnamon roll: 429 cal., 10g fat (5g sat. fat), 16mg chol., 311mg sod., 81g carb. (48g sugars, 1g fiber), 5g pro.

Spiced Maple Mustard

PREP: 15 min. • **COOK:** 30 min. + chilling • **MAKES:** 1 cup

1	tsp. whole allspice
¾	cup plus 3 Tbsp. water, divided
½	cup white vinegar
¼	cup maple syrup
1	Tbsp. all-purpose flour
1	Tbsp. cornstarch
2	tsp. ground mustard
1	tsp. ground turmeric
¾	tsp. salt

1. Place allspice on a double thickness of cheesecloth. Gather corners of cloth to enclose the seasonings; tie securely with string. In a small bowl, mix ¾ cup water, vinegar and maple syrup until blended; set aside. In a small saucepan, mix flour, cornstarch, mustard, turmeric, salt and remaining water until smooth. Gradually whisk in vinegar mixture. Add the spice bag. Simmer over medium heat until thickened, 5-10 minutes, stirring occasionally.
2. Discard spice bag. Transfer to a covered container; cool slightly. Refrigerate until cold. Store in refrigerator for up to 1 month.

1 Tbsp.: 19 cal., 0 fat (0 sat. fat), 0 chol., 111mg sod., 4g carb. (3g sugars, 0 fiber), 0 pro.

Pepper-Crusted Sirloin Roast

PREP: 15 min. • **BAKE:** 2 hours + standing
MAKES: 16 servings

2	Tbsp. Dijon mustard
1	Tbsp. coarsely ground pepper
1	Tbsp. minced fresh mint or 1 tsp. dried mint
1	Tbsp. minced fresh rosemary or 1 tsp. dried rosemary, crushed
1	beef sirloin tip roast (4 lbs.)

1. Preheat oven to 350°. Mix first 4 ingredients.
2. Place roast on a rack in a roasting pan; spread with mustard mixture. Roast until desired doneness (a thermometer should read 135° for medium-rare, 140° for medium and 145° for medium-well), about 2 hours.
3. Remove from the oven; tent with foil. Let stand 15 minutes before slicing.

3 oz. cooked beef: 146 cal., 5g fat (2g sat. fat), 72mg chol., 78mg sod., 1g carb. (0 sugars, 0 fiber), 23g pro.
Diabetic exchanges: 3 lean meat.

Swiss Cheese Potatoes

PREP: 30 min. • **BROIL:** 5 min.
MAKES: 12 servings

8	large potatoes, peeled and cubed (about 4 lbs.)
1½	tsp. salt, divided
2	cups chopped celery
¾	cup chopped onion
1½	cups shredded Swiss cheese, divided
⅔	cup 2% milk
3	Tbsp. butter
¼	tsp. pepper

1. Place potatoes and 1 tsp. salt in a Dutch oven; add water to cover. Bring to a boil. Reduce heat; cook, uncovered, for 10 minutes. Add celery and onion; cook until vegetables are tender, 10-15 minutes. Drain; transfer to a large bowl.
2. Mash potato mixture, gradually adding ¾ cup cheese, milk, butter, pepper and remaining salt. Transfer to a greased 8-in. square baking pan; sprinkle with remaining cheese. Broil 3-4 in. from the heat until cheese is lightly browned, 5-8 minutes.

¾ **cup:** 235 cal., 8g fat (5g sat. fat), 21mg chol., 368mg sod., 36g carb. (4g sugars, 3g fiber), 7g pro.

Polly's Perfect Potato Soup

PREP: 15 min. • **COOK:** 30 min.
MAKES: 8 servings

6	medium potatoes (about 4 lbs.), peeled and cu bed
3	cups whole milk
½	cup heavy whipping cream
2	Tbsp. unsalted butter
1	garlic clove, minced
1¼	tsp. kosher salt
1	tsp. coarsely ground pepper
½	tsp. seasoned salt
6	green onions, thinly sliced
	Shredded cheddar cheese and crumbled bacon, optional

1. Place potatoes in a large stockpot or Dutch oven; cover with cold water. Bring to a boil. Cook, uncovered until very tender, 20-25 minutes; drain well, reserving 1 cup liquid.

2. Return potatoes to stockpot or Dutch oven; mash until desired consistency. Return the pan to heat and add milk, heavy cream, butter, garlic and seasonings; heat on medium-low until heated through, 5-10 minutes, adding reserved cooking liquid to thin soup to desired consistency. Serve warm. Top with green onions. If desired, sprinkle with cheese and bacon.

1¼ **cups:** 230 cal., 11g fat (7g sat. fat), 34mg chol., 444mg sod., 28g carb. (7g sugars, 2g fiber), 6g pro.

Chocolate Pecan Skillet Cookie

PREP: 15 min. • **BAKE:** 35 min. • **MAKES:** 12 servings

- 1 cup butter
- 1 cup sugar
- 1 cup packed brown sugar
- 2 large eggs, room temperature
- 2 tsp. vanilla extract
- 3 cups all-purpose flour
- 1½ tsp. baking soda
- ½ tsp. kosher salt
- 1 cup 60% cacao bittersweet chocolate baking chips
- 1 cup chopped pecans, toasted
  Vanilla ice cream, optional

1. Preheat oven to 350°. In a 12-in. cast-iron skillet, heat butter in oven as it preheats. Meanwhile, in a large bowl, stir together sugar and brown sugar. When the butter is almost melted, remove skillet from oven and swirl butter until completely melted. Stir butter into sugar mixture; set skillet aside.
2. Beat eggs and vanilla into sugar mixture. In another bowl, whisk together flour, baking soda and salt; gradually beat into sugar mixture. Stir in chocolate chips and nuts. Spread mixture into buttered skillet.
3. Bake until toothpick inserted in center comes out with moist crumbs and top is golden brown. Serve warm, with vanilla ice cream if desired.

1 serving: 528 cal., 27g fat (13g sat. fat), 72mg chol., 378mg sod., 69g carb. (43g sugars, 3g fiber), 6g pro.

Sweet Corn Muffins

PREP: 10 min. • **BAKE:** 25 min. • **MAKES:** 1 dozen

- 1½ cups all-purpose flour
- 1 cup sugar
- ¾ cup cornmeal
- 1 Tbsp. baking powder
- ½ tsp. salt
- 2 large eggs, room temperature
- ½ cup shortening
- 1 cup 2% milk, divided

In a bowl, combine the dry ingredients. Add eggs, shortening and ½ cup of milk; beat for 1 minute. Add the remaining milk; beat just until blended. Fill paper-lined muffin cups three-fourths full. Bake at 350° until muffins test done, 25-30 minutes.

1 muffin: 254 cal., 10g fat (3g sat. fat), 33mg chol., 241mg sod., 38g carb. (18g sugars, 1g fiber), 4g pro.

HANDCRAFTED WITH LOVE

Tree Ornaments

Make lasting memories of friends and family by turning their cards into a creative decoration.

WHAT YOU'LL NEED
- Holiday cards
- Card stock
- Decorative twine
- Decorative bead
- Circular craft punch
- Scissors
- Pencil
- Craft glue stick

DIRECTIONS
1. Using a 2½-in. circular craft punch, cut 20 circles from cards.
2. Cut a 2½-in. equilateral triangle from card stock.
3. Trace triangle on back of each circle and fold each side outward along the lines.
4. Line up 5 circles with the triangle shapes facing same direction and secure bent sides together in a row with craft glue. Repeat with another five circles. This creates the top and bottom of ball.
5. To create middle, line up remaining 10 circles and alternate triangle direction—one point up, one point down, etc. Secure with glue.
6. Cut a 24-in. piece of twine. Fold in half and string a decorative bead on it. Wrap the top, middle and bottom part of the ball around twine and glue each closed, leaving a length of twine hanging from bottom of the ball. Glue each row together to secure ball. Tie a knot in the bottom of twine.

Air Plant Wreath

Modern meets retro in a very merry,
low-maintenance, living wreath.

WHAT YOU'LL NEED

- Evergreen wreath
- Air plants
- Berry sprigs
- Ribbon

DIRECTIONS

1. Weave air plants into wreath. The example
   has 2 *Tillandsia tectorum*. Tuck in berry sprigs.
2. Tie ribbon around top of wreath to hang.

Stick Reindeer

You know Dasher and Dancer, but "Twiggy"
might just become the most famous one of all.

WHAT YOU'LL NEED

- Sticks of various sizes, from twigs to
  about 1 in. in diameter
- Small red bell
- Thumbtacks
- Miniature pine cones
- Handsaw or hand pruners
- Hot glue gun

DIRECTIONS

1. Cut a 1-in.-diameter stick to 3½ in. for the body. Cut
   a separate 1½-in.-long piece on a diagonal for the
   head. Cut 4 legs from small sticks about ¼ in. in
   diameter. Hot-glue to the body.
2. Hot-glue red bell to cut edge of head for a Rudolph
   nose. Push thumbtacks in for eyes, using hot glue if
   needed to keep in place. Hot-glue head to body.
3. Trim down thin twigs to look like antlers. Hot-glue
   antlers in place on top of head.
4. Add mini pine cones with hot glue for ears and a tail.

"*Don't judge each day by the harvest you reap but by the seeds that you plant.*"
— ROBERT LOUIS STEVENSON

Sunbeams fall over a wheat field near La Junta, Colorado.
PHOTO BY DAN BALLARD/
GETTY IMAGES